PENGUIN VEER

1965

Rachna Bisht Rawat is the author of six books published by Penguin Random House India, including the bestsellers *The Brave* and *Kargil*. She lives in Gurugram with Hukum, the bright-eyed, bushy-tailed golden retriever; an eclectic collection of books and music; and Manoj Rawat, the man in Olive Green who met her when he was a gentleman cadet at the Indian Military Academy and offered to be her comrade for life. Occasionally, they are visited by Saransh the Wise, who has moved out to explore the world on his own. She can be reached at rachnabisht@gmail.com. Her Instagram handle is @rachna_bishtrawat.

PRAISE FOR THE BOOK

'The author takes Indian military history out of the dry realm of official accounts that are based on General Staff studies and skilfully transforms them into stirring tales of valour and sacrifice in battle. Using first-hand interviews with veterans who helped create the history she writes about, she approaches her subject with a rare sensitivity and compassion, presenting the reader with an insight into war with a human face'—Sqn Ldr Rana T.S. Chhina (Retd), Secretary, United Service Institution Centre for Armed Forces Historical Research, New Delhi

'To the thousands of books already published on the 1965 India–Pakistan War, this is a valuable addition. For it focuses on some of the most famous battles fought and won, leading to the utter collapse of Pakistan's misadventure in the hope of wresting Kashmir from India. An additional merit of the book is that vivid accounts of battles are accompanied by a pen-portrait of the gallant heroes of each'—Inder Malhotra, noted military historian and author

1965

STORIES FROM THE SECOND INDO-PAK WAR

RACHNA BISHT RAWAT

PENGUIN
VEER

An imprint of Penguin Random House

PENGUIN VEER

USA | Canada | UK | Ireland | Australia
New Zealand | India | South Africa | China | Singapore

Penguin Veer is part of the Penguin Random House group of companies
whose addresses can be found at global.penguinrandomhouse.com

Published by Penguin Random House India Pvt. Ltd
4th Floor, Capital Tower 1, MG Road,
Gurugram 122 002, Haryana, India

First published by Penguin Books India 2015
Published in Ebury Press by Penguin Random House India 2019
Published in Penguin Veer by Penguin Random House India 2022

ISBN 9780143425373

Typeset in Adobe Garamond Pro by Manipal Digital Systems, Manipal
Printed at Replika Press Pvt. Ltd, India

www.penguin.co.in

For the men in olive green.
Writing their stories taught me what valour is.

Theirs not to reason why,
Theirs but to do and die

—*The Charge of the Light Brigade*

List of abbreviations

Nk	Naik
L/Nk	Lance Naik
Swr	Sawar

Awards

PVC	Param Vir Chakra
PVSM	Param Vishisht Seva Medal
MVC	Maha Vir Chakra
AVSM	Ati Vishisht Seva Medal
VrC	Vir Chakra
YSM	Yudh Seva Medal
SM	Sena Medal
VSM	Vishisht Seva Medal

Military terms

GOC	General Officer Commanding
CO	Commanding Officer
2IC	Second in Command
JCO	Junior Commissioned Officer
HQ	Headquarters
Div	Division
Coy	Company
FUP	Forming Up Place
BOP	Border Out Post
CFL	Cease-fire Line
POW	Prisoner of War
Para	Parachute
RCL	Recoilless

Contents

Foreword

This year marks the fiftieth anniversary of the historic 1965 War between India and Pakistan, and *1965: Stories from the Second Indo-Pak War* is an effort to commemorate it. On 1 September 1965, five decades ago, Pakistan invaded Chamb district in Jammu and Kashmir, triggering one of the largest armoured and infantry battles, and a series of operations and counter-operations. It was only the valour and sacrifice of the soldiers of the Indian Army that gave a befitting reply to the Pakistan invasion and ensured a resounding military victory for the nation.

Recounting the five major battles fought by the Indian Army, the narrative reconstructs the events of the 1965 Indo-Pak war, outlining details never revealed before through archival records and interviews with war veterans. The book features battles fought at Haji Pir, Asal Uttar, Barki, Dograi and Phillora, together with inspiring stories of our valiant war heroes in each battle.

Recording our war history is a way of celebrating the bravery of our soldiers who laid down their lives for the country and made us proud. It reminds us that freedom comes at a price and how important it is to cherish it.

It gives me great pleasure to write the foreword to *1965: Stories from the Second Indo-Pak War* by Rachna Bisht Rawat. I compliment the Indian Army for taking the initiative to bring out this useful and well-documented book. I hope the book will make you pause and think about the courage and sacrifice of our soldiers who defend our borders and ensure our freedom.

Jai Hind

New Delhi   Manohar Parrikar
3 August 2015   Minister of Defence

Introduction

In February 2015, I was in South Block to gift a copy of my first book, *The Brave: Param Vir Chakra Stories*, to the Vice Chief of the Army Staff, Lt Gen Philip Campose, along with Penguin editor Renu Agal. We were sitting in the office of the Additional Directorate General of Public Information, the dynamic Maj Gen Shokin Chauhan, YSM, SM, VSM (now Lt Gen), when he sprung a surprise on us. He wanted a book commemorating the five grittiest battles fought by the Indian Army in 1965. He wanted a well-researched book. And he wanted it in August, in time for the fiftieth anniversary of the war. This meant that I would have approximately four months to read, research, travel, interview and write 50,000 words; and Penguin would have just a month to edit, typeset, design and publish it. Renu and I looked at each other in alarm, had a hushed it-just-can't-be-done conversation, looked him firmly in the eye and found ourselves telling him we would do it. The General smiled. He had recruited two more soldiers. That was my first experience of how inspiring leadership can convince one to take on impossible tasks.

As I started researching the five battles, I realized that was what the 1965 war had been all about as well. Great leaders with a bold vision and inspired foot soldiers eager to prove themselves. That was all we needed to turn the tables in that war. Despite its military might and the latest world technology at its disposal, Pakistan had to bow before the Indian soldier's grit and determination to win.

All five battles in this book have been related by veterans who fought in 1965 and survived to tell the tale. Hearing their stories has been one of the most memorable experiences of my life. Amongst these brave soldiers was Dfr Vir Singh (Retd) of 4 Horse, whose flesh was charred off his bones by a Cobra missile that hit his tank. He spoke with great regard for his Squadron Commander Maj Bhupinder Singh, MVC, who too was severely burned in the same attack after they had destroyed many tanks in the Battle of Phillora. When the then Prime Minister of India Lal Bahadur Shastri visited a dying Maj Singh in the Army Base Hospital, Delhi, the officer had tears in his eyes. A touched Shastri told Maj Singh that tears didn't become a brave soldier like him. Maj Singh replied, 'Sir, I'm not pained because of any injury. I'm anguished that a soldier is not being able to salute his Prime Minister.' These were the sorts of incidents that stung my eyes and made writing the book much more that a literary exercise. In relating these tales of cold courage and determination, I learnt what valour truly is.

The book was done at breakneck speed. In these hectic months, I put my life on hold, spending my days travelling, meeting war heroes and researching in the United Service

Institute of India (USI) library, and my nights typing away at my computer. The Additional Director General of Public Information and his team of officers also made the book a priority. The book was being edited even as the chapters were being written. Pictures were being sourced, permissions sought, war diaries scanned. The book has maps certified by the ministry of defence and rare pictures acquired not just from Army archives but also from the personal albums of officers interviewed.

When you read it, I just want you to remember that there are many versions of history and what we read is not always what actually happened. War accounts are often exaggerated and overemphasized. I have tried to avoid doing that. These battles are narrated by those who fought them, so I feel this is the closest we could have got to the truth. The Army has been brutally honest in letting me include incidents where we were attacked by our own tanks in the fog of war or where battalions had to pull out of areas they had to fight hard to win, owing to confusion. Mistakes are made, even in wars, and I have not tried to hide that. In many cases, the bravery of the enemy has been acknowledged and applauded by our own soldiers. There are incidents where Pakistani Company Commanders have informed India about the bravery of an Indian soldier and vice versa. When I heard these stories, I was touched to the core. Soldiers respect bravery, even in the enemy.

This book takes you back fifty years to a battlefield from where many of our soldiers never returned. Those who did, came back with unbelievable stories of great courage and fortitude; some returned with disabilities they gracefully spend the rest of their lives with. I salute them all. I will end by saying that battle victories are not celebrated, they are commemorated. That is what this book aims to do. I hope you will read it in the spirit in which it has been written.

Rachna Bisht Rawat

The Battle of Haji Pir

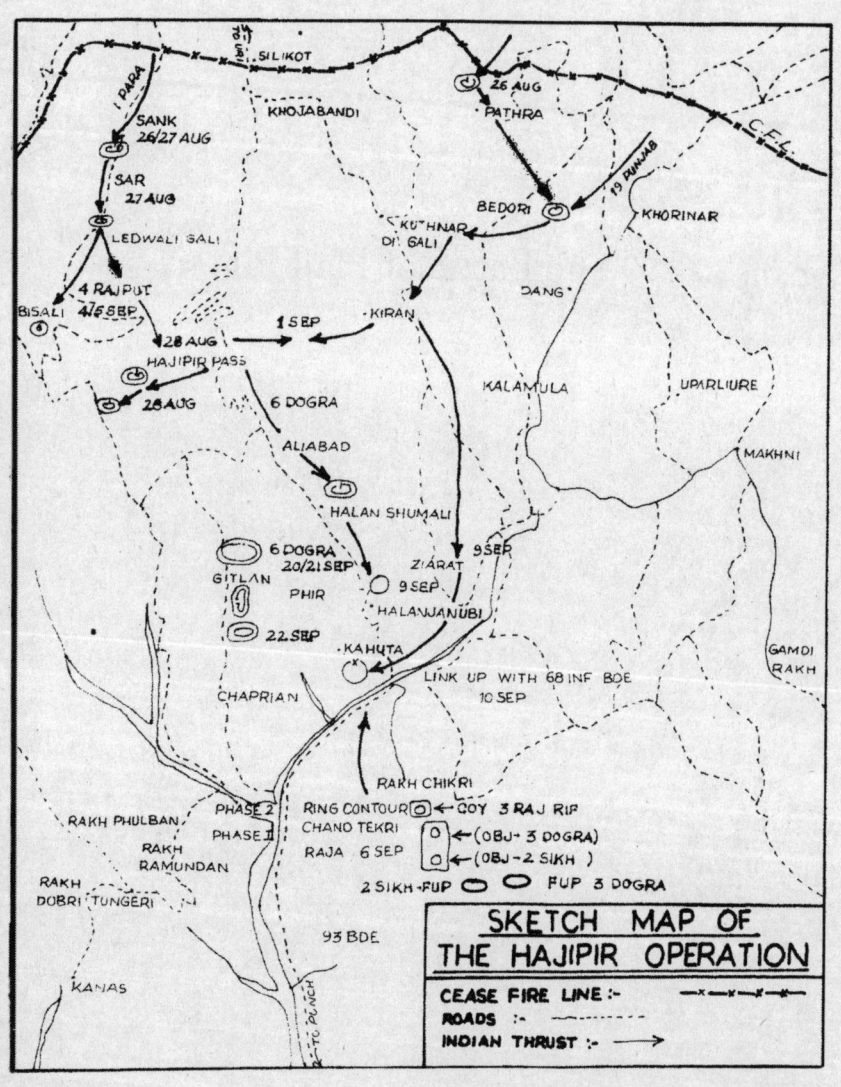

Courtesy: History Division, Ministry of Defence

Haji Pir Pass (8652 ft) is located south of Uri and about 8 km from the Cease-Fire Line. The Karachi Agreement of 1949 had given the pass to Pakistan and deprived India of the use of the Uri–Punch track. Neither side was allowed to go within 500 metres of the line. In early 1965, Pakistan's troops on the Cease-Fire Line started firing at India's supply convoys. Three of Pakistan's posts in the Kargil area overlooked the Srinagar–Leh highway. In early May, the troops holding these positions started firing on the highway and disrupting traffic. An angry India drove the Pakistanis out of their posts but soon after the agreement over the Rann of Kutch, the captured area was returned to Pakistan.

Even as the Prime Ministers of the two countries got involved in friendly diplomatic banter, Pakistan was devising an ingenious plot to annex Kashmir. It was planned that a large guerrilla force trained in Pakistan would be slipped across the Cease-Fire Line in small parties. The idea was to create anarchy in Srinagar, overthrow the administration and form a puppet government. When the Indian Army would take action against this, the Pakistan Army would attack in response to the puppet government's cry for help.

These guerrilla forces were named Gibraltar Forces and placed under the command of Maj Gen Akhtar Hussain Malik, a Divisional Commander in the Pakistan Army. In the first week of August 1965, the Gibraltar Forces entered Indian Kashmir at widely separated points along the 756-km Cease-Fire Line. They mostly travelled at night, crossed the jungles and climbed the hills. They would penetrate deep into the area and disperse in small batches. As they were dressed in loose phirans just like the locals—which also helped to conceal their guns—they blended in with the villagers, and some even managed to reach Srinagar. They started creating disturbances in the Valley by indulging in arson, looting and murder. Part of their plan was to capture the radio station, burn bridges and create roadblocks so that the area could be isolated from the rest of India. While the Indian Army took over from the state police, it was quickly understood that the only solution was to plug the invaders' point of entry. On 15 August, the Indian Army recaptured the three Pakistani posts it had occupied in May. A few days later the Pakistani artillery moved closer to the border and started intense shelling of the Indian positions near Tithwal, Uri and Punch. This is when the decision was made to take over Haji Pir Pass which was one of the routes being used by the infiltrators.

THE HAJI PIR STORY

Almost fifteen years have passed since the 1965 war. It is a crisp autumn day at Rustam post in the Uri sector on the Indian side of the Cease-Fire Line. A tall and handsome

Sikh officer, nearing fifty, looks across at Haji Pir Pass that stretches out on the Haji Pir bulge in all its magnificence. Memories of a dark, rain-splashed August night when the clouds had hung low over the hills and the paratroopers of 1 Para had climbed those treacherous slopes on all fours play out before his eyes. He doesn't say anything then, but later he would write about the nostalgia he felt at that moment in *Paratrooper* magazine:

> What a day it was, almost fifteen years ago on August 28, 1965 when, as a thirty five year old Major commanding two infantry companies, I had set foot on the Haji Pir pass. To gain that proverbial foothold my gallant men of 1st Para, the oldest battalion of the Indian Army, and I had to fight a bloody battle dislodging the resilient Pakistanis inch by inch. We all had immense satisfaction when the code word Chamak Tara, denoting our successful capture of the pass, was flashed to all the higher headquarters. It was a dream come true.

Lt Gen Ranjit Singh Dyal who was awarded a Maha Vir Chakra (MVC) for that gutsy operation succumbed to cancer a few years ago, but his comrades Brig Arvinder Singh (Retd), a young Company Commander in 1965, and Col J.S. Bindra, who was Battalion Adjutant then, remember the Battle of Haji Pir and recount it to me—event by event—as if it happened yesterday. The Bedori battle account, where 19 Punjab fought so valiantly, comes from conversations with Maj Gen J.R. Bhatti (Retd), who was Battalion Adjutant in 1965.

Battle plan

Once the decision was made that Haji Pir Pass would be taken from Pakistan so that the infiltration route that was being used to spark insurgency in Kashmir could be plugged, Lt Gen Harbaksh Singh, Army Commander, Western Command, tasked 68 Infantry Brigade with clearing the Haji Pir bulge of Pakistanis. The operation to attack and occupy Haji Pir was termed Op Bakshi, named after Brig Zorawar Chand Bakshi (better known as Zoru Bakshi), Brigade Commander of 68 Infantry Brigade. It was an indication of just how much faith the higher-ups reposed in him. Zoru Bakshi came up with a daring plan. The Indian Army would close on Haji Pir in a pincer-like move from the ridges on both sides and crush the enemy right there. It was to be a two-pronged attack.

Two of the identified attacking units already held pickets in the area and were thus familiar with the terrain. On one side of the nullah—holding pickets in Seb, Santra, Khiladare, Dhana, Chaukas, Chabak and Kaman ridges—was 1 Para, one of the oldest units of the Indian Army. On the other side was 19 Punjab—a new raising, barely a year old. It was decided that 1 Para would capture the western ridge of the pass which included Sank Peak (Point 9591), Sar and Ledwali Gali, while 19 Punjab would capture the eastern ridge, taking over a daunting feature called Bedori (12,330 ft). Once the shoulders of the pass were occupied, another battalion—4 Rajput—that had done exceedingly well in Kargil, would move in and capture Haji Pir.

It was a good plan. But sometimes even the best-laid of plans go awry. And sometimes, impossible victories are seized on the basis of sheer willpower and raw courage. Both these things were to happen in Haji Pir. However, on the dark, cloudy, rain-threatened night of 24–25 August, when Maj Ranjit Singh Dyal and the paratroopers of 1 Para had a hearty dinner, stocked a dry ration of *shakarpara*s and biscuits in their backpacks, laced up their boots, rammed on their helmets and began climbing for their first attack on Sank, they had no inkling of what destiny had in store for them.

It had been raining incessantly for two days. The attack that had initially been planned for 24 August had been postponed by twenty-four hours because the nullahs were in spate and the ground had turned soggy. But when the weather showed no sign of improvement on 25 August, orders were finally passed to launch the attack. Since Sank, which was occupied by the enemy, and Seb, where 1 Para was located, were almost at the same height, the war preparations were not hidden from the Pakistani soldiers. Both sides knew that a bloody confrontation was to happen soon.

The night of 25–26 August

The time is 10.30 p.m.; ominous dark clouds are hanging low over the grey mountains and the temperature has dropped sharply when the men of Alpha and Charlie companies, 1 Para, strap up their backpacks, sling their .303 bolt-action para rifles across their backs and start walking briskly through the undergrowth. They climb down to the nullah and cross it quickly, their muddy boots splashing in the water, and start their ascent, heading for Sank. The plan is to go stealthily and swiftly in the darkness of night and attack the enemy before first light, taking him by surprise.

The men are still climbing when the clouds break and the rain starts pouring down on them in thick sheets. They are soon soaked to the skin but ignore the weather conditions and keep walking, teeth grit, heads down. The ground under their feet is slippery and often they fall, but pick themselves up to begin climbing again. Since there is no direct track leading to the enemy position, the men take a frontal approach—a straight climb, difficult as well as dangerous. They pull themselves up by whatever they can grasp, trying to find boot-holds in the slippery mud. 'Unfortunately, they lost their way in the confusion created by the rain and the darkness. The post that they thought was right ahead and within easy reach suddenly seemed unattainable. The men had been walking for more than six hours and they were puzzled as to why they had not reached Sank yet,' remembers Col J.S. Bindra (Retd), who was Battalion Adjutant at the time.

Quite suddenly, the early hours of the morning ring out with the flash of machine-gun fire. The men of Alpha Company, who are ahead, are still trying to get a foothold on the slippery slope when the enemy guns start firing. They try to get a grip and fire back but are at a disadvantage. Men start falling to bullets and their cries of pain rend the air. Sank is held by more than one enemy company, supported by medium machine guns, and 3-inch and 4.2-inch mortars. The crafty enemy has been watching them climb up and starts firing the moment they come within range. Only one brave man manages to reach the top: it is paratrooper Lal Singh—one of the top athletes of the battalion. He is captured by the enemy, brutally butchered and his mutilated body thrown down. It is found by 1 Para much later. In an interview describing the battle many years later, Maj Dyal tells a magazine, 'He (the enemy) had seen us climbing up. He held his fire till we closed in and then opened up. A confusing battle ensued till 9.30 a.m. and the leading platoon suffered twenty-eight casualties. Our attack had failed and we were asked to break contact and pull back.'

The two attacking companies return. They are given covering fire by their battalion while they evacuate their casualties. Lal Singh cannot be traced and is given up as missing. Brig Arvinder Singh, who was Company Commander, Delta Company in 1965, remembers how the soldiers spent the morning of 26 August evacuating the injured, while the artillery pounded Sank through the day to make the enemy keep his head down. 'I saw Maj Dyal bringing injured soldiers down the steep slope on his back,' he says.

The second attack on Sank

On the night of 26–27 August, the battalion launches another attack. This time the attacking companies are Bravo (Dogras) led by Maj H.A. Patil and Delta (Ahirs) led by Maj Arvinder Singh. Maj Dyal is again at the helm of the attack. Avenge last night's defeat—that is the thought paramount in everybody's mind. 'We were raring to go; the men were full of *josh*. Maj Dyal had volunteered to come with us. He was thirty-five, a mature senior Major with fourteen years of experience behind him. I was twenty-four, Patil slightly older; we were plucked chickens with Majors' ranks on our shoulders,' Brig Singh recalls with a smile. This time the soldiers start climbing up in small groups. The artillery keeps pounding the peak to soften up the enemy. 'The ground was still slippery though it had stopped raining. We were climbing on all fours for the most part. We would slip and slide back, and again find a handhold and pull ourselves up; our faces and hands were smeared with grime, our uniforms were ripped but our spirit was intact as we kept climbing.'

No sooner do the attacking companies reach the base of the feature than the enemy troops come out of their trenches and start firing at them with automatic weapons. Forward Observation Officer Capt Naidu, who is accompanying them, helps direct the artillery fire. He adjusts the fire to deal with the surprise move of the enemy. The enemy suffers badly but the closeness of the artillery fire to 1 Para's own troops gives them some anxious moments.

The two companies keep inching their way up and at the crack of dawn the attack finally takes place. Since their medium and light machine guns have been silenced by the artillery fire, the enemy flees, leaving behind fifteen dead. 'We found the bodies of enemy soldiers and a lot of ammunition. It was obvious that the artillery fire had been on target and had caused much damage. By 7.30 a.m. we had captured Sank and given a success signal,' recounts Brig Singh.

The men decide to press forward and attack the two other posts further up the ridge. These are Sar and Ledwali

Gali. 'At 8 a.m. we received orders to attack the next post, Sar. As we moved farther along the narrow, rocky path on the ridge, the enemy saw us coming and opened fire. We fired back and kept advancing. We could see that there were around twelve enemy soldiers and they had made bunkers on that steep ridge. The route on which we were advancing was just a few yards wide and they could have just shot us at point-blank range, but fortunately that did not happen. They kept up their fire till the last moment and then fled. We could capture Sar without any casualties. The same thing was repeated as we advanced towards Ledwali Gali. The enemy kept firing at us even as they withdrew. The psyche of the Pakistanis is they are good fighters as long as they are winning, but if they start losing, they run,' he says. The end result of the quick and daring assault was that within three hours, Sank, Sar and Ledwali Gali had been captured by 1 Para. The objectives given to the battalion had effectively been met.

On the eastern ridge

The Uri–Punch bulge consists of rugged mountainous terrain with heights varying from 4000 ft to 12,000 ft. Above 8000 ft the peaks remain snow-covered for the most part of the year. At 12,330 ft Bedori is the highest point in the bulge. It dominates the bulge and overlooks the Uri sector.

According to Zoru Bakshi's plan, while 1 Para was to advance along Sank–Sar–Ledwali Gali, the other column comprising 4 Rajput and 19 Punjab was to advance along Point 10048–Point 11094–Bedori–Kuthnar di Gali–Haji

Pir Pass. The pincer-like twin arms would converge at Haji Pir.

The troops of 19 Punjab, entrusted with securing the firm base, also launched operations on 25 August to maintain the element of surprise. While 1 Para was unsuccessful in capturing Sank in the first attack, by 1.30 a.m. on 26 August, 19 Punjab had captured Pathra. However, 4 Rajput, that had been tasked with taking over Bedori, was not able to do so. The brave soldiers put up a tough fight at the risk of their lives but the post was on a craggy mountain, steep and insurmountable. Since it was a rocky area where digging trenches was difficult, the Pakistanis had made rough fortifications called *sangar*s from rocks and were firing from behind these. 'It was a rugged and precipitous terrain and the Pakistanis put up a solid defence. Bedori was almost impossible to capture,' says Col Bindra. Moreover, the route selected for the attack turned out to be more difficult than expected owing to the cliffs and hanging rocks. The 4 Rajput soldiers suffered heavy casualties and were forced to return. Brig Bakshi decided on 27 August to attempt Bedori once again with 7 Bihar and asked 19 Punjab to relieve 1 Para in the Sank area. But Lt Col (later Brig) Sampuran Singh, Commanding Officer of 19 Punjab, a proud soldier, was unwilling to accept such a passive role for his battalion. He volunteered to attack Bedori if he was permitted to choose his own direction of attack and got his way. A new route of attack was planned. Lt Col Sampuran Singh and his Adjutant Lt (later Maj Gen) J.R. Bhatti had earlier reconnoitred a route to Bedori that went through Kaunrali–Gagarhil–Bedori Springs. He decided that 19 Punjab would advance on that route.

Winning Bedori

It has been three days. The soldiers of 19 Punjab have been on the move since 25 August, carrying heavy loads that include mortars and ammunition, often in heavy rain—wet and shivering in the extreme cold—and, as they are human after all, fatigue has started setting in. The rations that they carried have run out in seventy-two hours and thereafter they have been living off the land, sending parties to fetch gram and maize from the fields 7000 ft below. Beyond that height no crops grow. An attempted airdrop of food has also fallen into a nullah on the enemy territory and the helpless and hungry soldiers just watch it lie there, and since there are no chances of retrieving it, they move on. It is to their credit, however, that when the orders come for them to go for another attack on Bedori, they do not flinch.

On the night of 27–28 August, the men walk down from Pathra, situated at a height of around 10,000 ft, to Uri, located at 4000 ft. Determined and drawing on their last reserves of stamina, they line up at Uri in their stone-ripped uniforms, their battle-scarred faces tough and resilient, and wait patiently for the trucks that will carry them to Kaunrali, located at about 4500 ft. Many of them close their eyes for a few moments of peace and rest during that 25-km journey. After the trucks unload them, they start yet another long walk. With quiet determination, they keep climbing through the day. Their objective is to reach Bedori Springs at 11,500 ft by last light on 28 August. Alpha Company has been left behind to relieve 1 Para at Sank. By midnight, Delta Company has secured a Forming Up Place (FUP) from where the attack will be launched. On their way to Bedori Springs, the battalion comes across 7 Bihar—whose attack on Bedori has also failed—returning with their casualties. It is demoralizing for the soldiers to watch dead and injured comrades being carried down the slopes, but they face their task with stoic resolve.

The approach that 19 Punjab takes to Bedori is so narrow that at a time only one company can go in for the attack. A two-phased attack is launched along the eastern approach. Bravo Company, led by Maj S.B. Verma, is the first to go. A brutal fight ensues and they manage to secure a part of the objective. Charlie Company, led by Maj Parminder Singh, then pushes in ruthlessly and completes the attack. Bedori is eventually taken over by 6 a.m. on 29 August. Victory has come to 19 Punjab after three failed attempts to take over Bedori. It is a victory seized by sheer fortitude and the will to do or die. Lt Col Sampuran Singh has delivered on his promise. In this operation 19 Punjab has marched man packed (carrying all their load which includes ration, ammunition, weapons, on their body) from a height of 10,000 ft to 4000 ft and then again to a height of 11,000 ft, and captured Bedori at 12,330 ft without taking a break. They have covered an unbelievable distance of 40 km on foot and 25 km in vehicles in a span of twenty-four hours.

But there is no time to wait for supplies as the key factor in the victory is the element of surprise. The battalion prepares to move on to Kuthnar di Gali, its next objective. Not only are the soldiers tired, they are also hungry, having gone for hours together without proper food. There is an interesting twist to the tale. Maj (later Lt Gen) L.S. Rawat, Brigade Major, 161 Infantry Brigade, who is at Rampur, happens to be listening in on the wireless message that says 19 Punjab is without food. He immediately takes matters in his own hands and, with the assistance of a local Congress official, manages to dispatch puris for 700 soldiers to Bedori. Unfortunately, the battalion has already moved on to Kuthnar di Gali by then, but one company that has been left behind at Bedori gets an unexpected meal. It is only after capturing Kuthnar di Gali and Kiran on 1 September that 19 Punjab links up with 1 Para at Haji Pir Pass and the battle-weary soldiers get to eat a proper meal.

Their task is, however, not over yet. On 9 September, they make a bold daylight attack on a post called Ziarat, and later, Delta Company of 19 Punjab, along with one company of 6 Dogra, secures a tricky post called Gittian in the Kahuta heights where a brutal hand-to-hand fight ensues. Both the Company Commanders—Maj Ranbir Singh of 19 Punjab and Major Lalli of 6 Dogra—lay down their lives in this fierce battle and are awarded Vir Chakras (VrC) posthumously. In these operations the unit also loses twenty-one Other Ranks.

Thereafter, an attack on Point 8777 is launched by Charlie Company under Maj Parminder Singh. The company has captured part of the objective when it is dislodged by an enemy counter-attack. The 19 Punjab is in the process of regrouping to launch another attack on Point 8777, when ceasefire is declared. The war is effectively over. During the exchange of bodies of soldiers after the ceasefire, Maj Rizvi of 20 Punjab, Pakistan Army, who was defending Point 8777, makes a special mention of the bravery with which L/Nk Lakha Singh of C Company fought. After he ran out of ammunition, Lakha used his bayonet to kill enemy soldiers. When that broke, he took off his helmet and started knocking men out with it, Maj Rizvi tells the 19 Punjab officers.

Maj Gen J.R. Bhatti (Retd), who was Battalion Adjutant at that time, still remembers how Lakha's eyes used to shine like a tiger's. Now settled in Meerut, Maj Gen Bhatti recalls, 'Lakha was in my company and my platoon. He was a Himachali; a big-built man, stout and sturdy, courageous and fearless. Maj Rizvi told us that he had tried his best to save Lakha's life by shouting out orders to his men not to kill the unarmed soldier who was fighting so valiantly with his helmet, but in the chaos of war, his orders were lost and Lakha was shot dead.'

Lakha's act of bravery was recognized by the government and he was awarded a Vir Chakra posthumously, while another Vir Chakra was awarded to Sepoy Dev Raj. Dev Raj was on a medium machine-gun detachment and continued to fire with no regard for his own life despite both his comrades being injured. Within a span of one month, Lt Col Sampuran Singh was decorated with the Maha Vir Chakra and the Vir Chakra. The young unit's achievements were recognized and it was given the Battle Honour Bedori and the Theatre Honour Haji Pir.

The long climb up to Haji Pir

The task that had been assigned to 1 Para was effectively over at 11 a.m. on 27 August. The paratroopers were, however, itching for more action. 'Through our binoculars we looked at Haji Pir Pass; we could not see any activity there,' recollects Brig Singh. 'We were at 10,000 ft. If we went down and crossed the Hyderabadi nullah and climbed up again, we could reach Haji Pir which was at 8652 ft. We were confident and knew the area well. Maj Dyal discussed it with me and we both felt that we could attack Haji Pir.

'Maj Dyal called up our Commanding Officer Lt Col Prabhjinder Singh and said, "I am ready, my troops are fit and we are in a position to go up to Haji Pir, sir, if we are given the permission to do so."' When Col Prabhjinder Singh was convinced, he in turn called up the Brigade and offered that 1 Para could attack Haji Pir. After almost two hours of thought and discussions, Gen Zoru Bakshi gave the go-ahead. Around 2 p.m. on 27 August, Maj Dyal got the orders to launch the attack on Haji Pir. What had been planned as a brigade-level attack was being taken on by a single company.

Since Alpha Company had lost many men in the first attack on Sank, Maj Dyal took along with him one platoon of Delta Company as well. These men were led by a Junior Commissioned Officer—Sub Arjan Singh—who was known for his grit and courage. Within half an hour of receiving orders, the men, numbering around 100, climbed down from Ledwali Gali, walked through the forest for around five hours and reached the Hyderabadi nullah late in the evening. They then waded through its ice-cold waters and reached the other side with trousers, socks and shoes sodden. 'We were used to the terrain, we knew exactly how cold the water could be, so it was not very difficult for the men,' says Brig Singh. Once they were on the other side, the men did not lose any time and started the long climb to Haji Pir Pass.

The assault on Haji Pir

Gen Dyal's reminiscences, courtesy *Paratrooper* magazine:

> I was asked to lead a strong company comprising men of Alpha and Delta companies and capture the pass. The singular distinction conferred on us sent our morale sky high despite the meager rations of dampened shakarparas and biscuits which we had been consuming since we parted company with the administrative echelon on August 25. We consumed the last of it around noon on August 27 and were on our way down the Hyderabadi nallah. The enemy brought some plunging and inaccurate fire on us. Obviously, it was ineffective. Heavens were happy with us and suddenly came the rains which in their wake brought low hanging clouds providing us the much needed camouflage. The enemy could not locate us anywhere.

Though the night was cold and the soldiers were drenched from their walk through the nullah and the rain, they were full of energy. Their earlier successes had filled them with confidence and even though this was their second night without sleep, they did not show any sign of fatigue. Maj

Dyal had not slept for three nights but his physical fitness was legendary. The fact that he was leading them filled the soldiers with even greater confidence.

On their climb up to the pass, the soldiers came across a *behak*, a hut which used a side of the mountain as a wall. Maj Dyal noticed some movement there and, finding it suspicious, he asked his men to surround it. When the occupants were asked to come out with their hands raised, they turned out to be a Captain of the Pakistan Army and eleven soldiers. From the Pakistani officer's pocket, the paratroopers retrieved a sketch of the location of 1 Para. On interrogation, the Captain confessed that the small party had been tasked with raiding 1 Para mess. They also found in his pocket a letter addressed to the Pakistan Army Chief, from which they came to know that he had asked for permission to go and see his dying father but had been sent on this mission instead. He was dejected and disgruntled, and had written to the chief saying he wanted to quit.

The enemy soldiers were disarmed and used as load bearers, and the paratroopers continued their climb to Haji Pir. Most of the time they had to climb on all fours since the rain had made the ground under their feet slushy. Around 4.30 a.m., they hit the Uri–Punch track; the pass was still around 10 km farther up. Maj Dyal told his soldiers to rest so that their energy could be conserved for the ensuing battle. They huddled together in the darkness for two hours, the rain beating down on their heads and trailing down their backs.

According to the battalion war diary:

No one had any blankets or warm clothing. Most of the men were carrying only waterproof capes. Once the orders to halt were given, everyone snuggled in small groups under overhanging rocks, leaning trees or even in the open, with heads down and the rain beating on their backs.

In the morning they came under medium machine-gun fire from the western shoulder of the pass. Leaving a platoon to deal with it, Maj Dyal led the rest of the soldiers to the right shoulder of the pass and then rolled down on to Haji Pir Pass. The suddenness of their daring assault flustered the enemy completely and they fled in confusion. By 10 a.m. on 28 August, Haji Pir Pass had been taken. The victory signal of 'Chamak Tara' roared on the wireless and fell on Zoru Bakshi's delighted ears; there was jubilation all around. All India Radio announced it to the country and within an hour of the news breaking, the Corps Commander declared a Maha Vir Chakra for Maj Ranjit Singh Dyal. The Tricolour was hoisted at Haji Pir; however, it was an insult Pakistan was not expected to take lying down and, instead of celebrating their victory, the paratroopers got down to preparing for a retaliatory attack. Maj Dyal immediately asked for reinforcements.

The Battle of Ring Contour

'On 28 August, around 10 a.m., we got orders to go and reinforce Maj Dyal's company. We went down to the nullah,

A shared toothbrush, two mountain goats and *puri alu*

Of the five officers at Haji Pir, Maj Dyal was the only one carrying a toothbrush. Since the operation stretched over days, the men went without brushing their teeth. Brig Arvinder Singh remembers how he was looking on wistfully one day while Maj Dyal was brushing. A magnanimous Maj Dyal offered his toothbrush to Maj Singh, who used it to brush his teeth and in turn passed it on to Capt Vaswani. Ultimately, all five officers used the same toothbrush and awaited some food. The starving jawans had caught two goats that they skinned and cooked in some *paraat*s they had found in a deserted *bashan* or hut. They had also found a little salt which was not enough for all the men. So the officers were given the salted partially cooked meat, while the jawans ate the rest without salt.

On the morning of 31 August, Flight Lt L.K. Dutta (actor Lara Dutta's father), Maj Singh's course mate posted in Srinagar, came to know that he was at Haji Pir without any food. He volunteered to take some food there for the stranded soldiers. As it was a cloudy day, the helicopter could not land but he airdropped the food packets. The soldiers, who had not eaten fresh food since 25 August, had a feast when they opened the packets to find *puri alu* inside.

climbed up and reached Haji Pir on 29 August around 4 a.m. It wasn't first light yet,' says Brig Singh. The day passed peacefully but as night fell, the officers became wary that a counter-attack from the enemy could come any time. A twenty-man platoon was sent up to the Ring Contour area and they returned with the startling information that the enemy could be observed gathering there in large numbers. Maj Singh left at 4.30 a.m. on 30 August with two platoons to ascertain this for himself. He reached there just as day was breaking and realized that the information had been correct. After Haji Pir was lost, the Pakistanis had started building up their troops at Ring Contour, which was a feature located 1.4 km south-west of the pass.

On the ridge ahead, they could see as many as thirty-five Pakistani soldiers dressed in khaki. 'Some of them had helmets on, while others were digging trenches. We knew that if we did not react immediately, they would attack Haji Pir and, since they were at a height, they would be at an advantage.' Brig Singh says he had a split second to decide whether to attack or to withdraw. He decided to be audacious and attack. 'It was our fifth day of operations; the radio batteries had no charge and there was no way I could have spoken to Maj Dyal. When I had left, there had been an understanding between us that if I needed help, he would come up. I decided we would go for the kill.'

Shouting out the Ahir war cry 'Kishan Maharaj ki Jai', Maj Singh and his men charged at the enemy soldiers. Since they were not fully prepared to face an assault, the Pakistanis were taken by surprise. A bloody confrontation—which is called the Battle of Ring Contour—followed. The soldiers fired at each other, grenades were flung, and the cries of the dying and wounded filled the air. Finally, it came down to a hand-to-hand fight where soldiers were bayoneting each other and blood stained the rocky heights. The ferociousness of the battle did not daunt the soldiers in the least, remembers Brig Singh. He cites an incident when, in his enthusiasm as a young Company Commander, he overtook the scouts section led by Hav Umrao Singh, a brave Ahir. 'He pointed his gun at me and said, "Get back! How dare you go ahead of me!" and I had to reluctantly let him go first.' Soon after, Hav Umrao Singh and the scout next to him fell to machine-gun fire. Delta Company lost seven men in the Battle of Ring Contour, while the number of wounded was twenty-two. A mortar shrapnel that ripped past Maj Singh tore off the bulk of his calf muscle, making him stagger to the ground. Despite not being able to walk, he took over the light machine gun of a dead comrade and, along with the twenty-nine surviving men of his company, kept the enemy at bay.

He remembers how paratrooper Hira Lal was hit by a burst of fire, yet continued to hold on to his grenade gun despite his intestines hanging out of a fatal stomach wound. 'Concerned, I stopped next to him. "*Sahab, maine mar jana hai, tu meri parvah mat kar, aage ja* (Sahab, I am going to die; you keep going)," he said. I moved on; he probably fired one more grenade and then collapsed and closed his eyes forever.'

Meanwhile, at Haji Pir, Maj Dyal heard the shots and saw gunfire lighting up the sky. Realizing that a tough battle was on, he decided to climb up with a small force that he had at his command. He reached Ring Contour in an hour and a half, and saw Maj Singh lying there with his leg nearly blown off, yet bravely handling a light machine gun. He stopped next to him to speak a few words of encouragement. While he was sitting there, a machine-gun burst hit his Sten gun on its housing and bullets went through his Denison smock. He was miraculously saved. That gun and the bullet-riddled Denison smock are prized exhibits at the 1 Para mess in Nahan.

Face-off

Brig Arvinder Singh remembers how in the 1971 war, when his Delta Company captured fourteen Pakistanis and they were presented before him for interrogation in the morning, one of them asked him in chaste Punjabi, '*Sahab, ji tu Haji Pir Pass te si? (Sahab, were you at Haji Pir Pass?)*' When he replied in the affirmative, the cheeky Pakistani POW jubilantly told him, '*Tussi Major de Major hi reh gaye, main te Lance Naik se Havildar ban gaya* (You have remained a Major, while I've become a Havildar from a Lance Naik).'

The battle raged through the day. The enemy made repeated attempts to take back Ring Contour but the gutsy soldiers of Delta Company retaliated each time. They kept losing men but stuck on with dogged determination until reinforcements reached them in the evening. The post was finally taken.

The injured soldiers lay there for eight hours waiting for reinforcements to reach them. Respite finally came on the evening of 30 August. The next morning, makeshift stretchers were designed by tying sheets between two poles, and the injured were evacuated. Evacuation from those heights was not an easy task. Brig Singh remembers how the battalion Subedar Major rounded up locals from nearby homes to help carry the stretchers. 'Eight young men were employed for each stretcher. Four would carry the stretcher, while the other four would walk alongside and take over when the first four got tired. It took them the whole of the next day to carry us down to Uri.' Maj Singh's wound was cleaned and dressed in a makeshift advance dressing station inside a tent. The excruciating pain he felt subsided only after a morphine shot was administered. He was evacuated to Army Base Hospital, Srinagar. From there he was shifted to Military Hospital, Agra. It took him several years to bounce back to perfect health but he has no regrets. 'We are very proud of what we did,' he says. 'We are also very proud of Gen Dyal. Normally, a battalion second in command [2IC] is supposed to be in the rear but here was a 2IC who was fighting every battle.'

The bravery of 1 Para in the capture of Haji Pir was duly recognized. It was awarded the Battle Honour Haji Pir. Maj Dyal was decorated with the Maha Vir Chakra, Hav Umrao Singh was awarded a Vir Chakra posthumously, while Capt Madan Mohan Pal Singh Dhillon and Sub Arjan Singh received the Sena Medal for conspicuous gallantry during the operations.

Gen Dyal's recap in *Paratrooper* on being awarded the Maha Vir Chakra:

> Our 1st Para became the blue-eyed *paltan* of the nation. The Prime Minister had a special word of appreciation for us. Cooke Sahab *ki* Paltan (as 1 Para was known at the time of its raising) had displayed a fine sense of esprit-de-corps be it in fighting against a resilient enemy or catching mountain goats after the fighting to satisfy our three-day-old hunger. And in recognition of our gallantry as the President of India pinned the Maha Vir Chakra on my chest, my heart went out to my comrades in arms who became martyrs on Ring Contour to secure the Haji Pir Pass. They gave their today for our tomorrow.

Shock to Pakistan

The occupation of the Haji Pir bulge plugged an important route of entry into Jammu and Kashmir for the raiders. Not only did it neutralize Pakistan's main bases of infiltration but it also snapped the physical contact between Pakistan and the invading guerrillas. Prime Minister Lal Bahadur Shastri made a bold statement on 3 September. 'As a measure of self-defence we had to take action to occupy strategic posts, cross the Cease-Fire Line in order to blast the roots of the infiltrators,' he said. This was a big shock to Pakistan who believed that India would not cross the International Border under any circumstances. However, it is widely felt that India lost in Tashkent what it won on the battlefield. The Haji Pir bulge, where so many battalions had fought so valiantly and so many brave soldiers had lost their lives, was given back to Pakistan in 1966 after the Tashkent Declaration. Col Bindra remembers how his soldiers had tears in their eyes when they finally evacuated Haji Pir since they had seen their comrades dying in that battle.

. . .

Around 2 p.m. on 27 August 1965, MAJ RANJIT SINGH
DYAL gets orders to launch the attack on Haji Pir. What
had been planned as a brigade-level attack is now being
taken on by a single company. The suddenness of the
daring assault he leads flusters the enemy completely
and they flee in confusion. By 10 a.m. on 28 August,
Haji Pir Pass is taken.

Lt Gen Ranjit Singh Dyal
Maha Vir Chakra, Param Vishisht Seva Medal

The Sikh paratrooper in the olive green uniform and red turban is standing ramrod straight. In his dark-brown eyes flecked with amber, there is uncertainty. He has been marched up to his battalion 2IC Maj Ranjit Singh Dyal. A tall, broad-shouldered sardar with casual confidence stamped all over his persona, Maj Dyal raises his head at the boot stomp and takes in with his dark flashing eyes the soldier's crisp salute and 'Ram Ram, sahab'.

'*Tune ek civilian ko apni dah se maar diya?* (Have you killed a civilian with your machete?)' he asks, his voice cold with fury. '*Ladai ho gayi thi, sahab ji* (We'd had a fight, sir),' the jawan replies, his eyes lowered. Dyal continues to glare at him. Since 1 Para has already received attack orders, with notice to move shortly, there is no time to hold a regular court of inquiry. '*Jis dah se tune us aadmi ko mara hai, usi dah ko lekar ab ladai mein chal. Apni bahaduri mujhe wahan dikhana* (Now carry the machete with which you killed that man and fight the battle with it. Show me your bravery there),' Maj Dyal tells the guilty soldier and, with a curt nod of his head, dismisses him. Orders to that effect are passed to Battalion Adjutant Capt J.S. Bindra, a young man in his early twenties.

Fifty years later, seventy-two-year-old Col Bindra sits in his Chandigarh residence (chairs pulled close to a plug point so that my dying cell battery can be charged while I record his interview) and chuckles as he recalls this incident. 'When we went to war, that soldier's gun was taken away from him. He took up the challenge with spirit, saying, "*Sahab ne jo keh diya karenge* (I will do what sir has told me to)." He went for the attack with the machete he used for clearing bushes, fought bravely and, wonder of wonders, returned safe too,' smiles the retired paratrooper. 'That was the kind of man Dyal was,' he remembers fondly. 'Not only was he brave himself; he also inspired bravery.'

Maj Dyal's stories of courage are legendary. Every man who knew him at some point and in some capacity can relate at least one. Brig Arvinder Singh (Retd), who was a twenty-four-year-old Company Commander under Maj Dyal during the Battle of Haji Pir, recounts two. The first story he tells me concerns Maj Harsh Yadav, Company Commander, Alpha Company, who had just gone on leave for his wedding when the battalion got orders to attack. 'All leaves were cancelled and those who had already left were given recall orders on radio. Maj Dyal requested the Commanding Officer that since Yadav had gone to get married, he should be allowed to stay back. When the Commanding Officer asked him who would command Alpha Company in his absence, Maj Dyal—who was the battalion 2IC at that time—volunteered to do it. A telegram was shot off to Yadav saying he could ignore the radio recall and continue with his leave,' Brig Singh says.

The second story comes from the first attack on Sank that 1 Para's Alpha and Charlie companies conducted on the night of 25 August. The soldiers lost their way and were spotted by the enemy when day broke. 'Our men came under heavy fire; since the enemy was sitting at a height, we suffered heavy casualties and had to return. Maj Dyal carried injured soldiers down the steep slope on his back. As the battalion 2IC, he did not have to do it but he did it anyway. His fitness level was superb and he was a man of immense courage,' Brig Singh remembers. That same night another attack was planned by the battalion, this time with Bravo and Delta companies, giving a break to the companies that had gone the night before; Maj Dyal again volunteered to lead, disregarding the fact that he hadn't slept at all.

This quality of Maj Dyal's is recognized by his friend Brig Kuldeep Singh Chandpuri, also a Maha Vir Chakra from the Battle of Longewala in 1971, on which the Sunny Deol film *Border* is based. 'In the Infantry School, Mhow, we teach Army officers motivation,' he says. 'Taking a lecture is easy, but in real life it is very difficult to motivate people. In war, when death is imminent, it becomes even more difficult. The only way to do it is by setting a personal example. Dyal was one of the few people who could do it. You must remember that he was the son of Sardar Bahadur Risaldar Ram Singh Dyal, a very brave man himself; not only that, he was also

OBI, at that time known as Officer of British India. It's a rare distinction that father and son were both gallantry award-winners.'

A born leader

Ranjit Singh Dyal was born on 15 November 1928 in Burma where his father, Sardar Bahadur Risaldar Ram Singh Dyal, was then serving. Soon after, his mother came back to India and settled down in a tiny village called Kante which lies in Una district of Himachal Pradesh, a little ahead of Anantpur Saheb. This was the place where Ranjit spent his childhood. Accompanied by the other boys from his village, he would walk five miles for his classes every day. After school got over, he would race his friends back, his colourful *patka* flashing in the late afternoon sun. He would stop to pick wildflowers and stuff them in his shirt pocket, and then he would race them again, easily beating boys older than him.

Ranjit was a spirited kid and in his gusto he would sometimes pull a child's hair leaving him in tears, tug at someone's shirt making the buttons pop open or wrestle someone in the mud, proclaiming his victory by sitting astride his stomach gleefully. The complaints would reach his exasperated mother who had six other children to take care of. Finally a day came when, fed up with her naughty son, she packed his bags, took him by the hand and boarded a bus to Jalandhar, where his father was then posted. She handed the errant Ranjit over to him saying he had become too difficult for her to handle.

Ris Maj Ram Singh decided to discipline his son and immediately got him admitted to the King George Royal Indian Military College boarding school in Jalandhar cantonment. Ranjit took to his new school very well and soon became its head boy. His schoolmates would later remember how he would send them back if he found that their turbans did not have the mandatory six folds. It was there that he began to hone his leadership quality. His ability to take charge and assume command stood him in good stead when he joined the Indian Military Academy. He got his commission on 12 September 1948 at the age of twenty and joined 1 Para (Punjab). In physical fitness he could match the best soldiers easily; to add to it, he was bold and courageous by temperament and had the strength of character to stand by what he believed in. 2Lt Ranjit Singh Dyal was headed for big things in life. He would go on to command his unit, become the Army Commander, then General Officer Commanding-in-Chief, and later the governor of both Puducherry and Andaman and Nicobar. Yet what he is best known for is that he was one of our first Maha Vir Chakra awardees in the early days of the 1965 war, when India was still smarting from the reverses suffered in the 1962 war and an initial setback in the western sector.

His profile would not be complete without recounting an incident that few people know about. Also from the 1965 war, it defines him completely.

After 1 Para's first attack on Sank failed miserably and the attacking companies returned with high casualties, the Commanding Officer of the unit was sacked by the higher authorities. Dyal, being the 2IC, was told to take over the unit. By the time these orders came, he had led his companies and captured the coveted Haji Pir Pass. However, he refused to take over, saying he would not do it under those circumstances as he did not agree that the failed attack reflected on his Commanding Officer's professional competence. He continued as the 2IC and it was much later and after much persuasion that he finally agreed to command his battalion. 'How many men would take a stand like that, particularly when it was benefiting them?' asks Col Bindra as he relates the story to me. 'Very few,' he answers himself.

Love at first sight

Dyal's stories of courage and fortitude were legendary. Right from the beginning, he was known for being a battle-hardy soldier and a hardcore bachelor. Younger officers, sitting in the mess with a glass of beer, had often wondered if he would ever marry and the conversation would generally end on the consensus that he probably wouldn't. He was in his forties when he fell in love and proved them wrong. Mrs Birender Kaur Dyal nostalgically relates the story of their first meeting in Samba. She was twenty-seven, and was visiting her sister and brother-in-law, an Air Force officer posted at Samba, when Ranjit Singh Dyal saw her for the first time. It was at a dinner organized at Samba for the Army and the Air Force. She was tall, frail and pretty, undergoing her teacher's training at St Bede's, Shimla, looking a little lost in the crowd that evening. He was forty-three, already a brigadier, and had seen action on the battlefield in 1962, 1965 and then again in 1971.

'When he saw me, he walked over to us and asked my brother-in-law, "Why are you hiding your pretty *sali*?"'

Mrs Dyal laughs at the recollection, adding modestly, 'Though of course, I'm not that pretty.' A few days later, he directly told her sister that he was interested in getting married and she asked her father, Karam Singh Kirti, a freedom fighter from Punjab and also an MLA, to meet the suitor. When the old man came down to Samba, he was impressed with not only the credentials of his daughter's suitor, but also his honesty. 'He told my father he got only Rs 1200 as salary and asked him if his daughter would be able to manage with that amount, impressing him completely.' Birender too was floored by the charm of this handsome, decorated soldier who was so full of life and, to top it all, was a paratrooper who could drop down from the skies on the wings of a parachute. And so the man who people thought would never get married, suddenly had a beautiful young wife, much to the delight of his battalion who had given up on him.

Mrs Dyal relates to me one of the many beautiful memories he left her with. 'Being the last one on the dance floor with a whisky glass balanced on his forehead, he would chide me if I protested that I was tired of dancing. "You are much younger than me, how can you be tired?" he would say and pull me back to the dance floor.' After parties, he would insist she drive the Fiat car they had bought for the princely sum of Rs 17,000 soon after their marriage. 'He would joke that he was a Brigade Commander who was used to chauffeur-driven cars and I would complain to him that he had married me just because he wanted a driver for his car.' Right up to the time when he became the governor of Puducherry and then of Andaman and Nicobar, he would insist that she make his chapatis. '"*Us ek chapati mein mujhe mazaa aa jaata hai*

(That single chapati gives me joy)," he would say. He had so much love for his battalion that when he visited Nahan, where 1 Para was located, even as a governor, he would insist on staying with the Commanding Officer. "We are family, I'm going to stay with you. I won't stay in a VIP guest house," he would say.'

The olive-green bond

Gen Dyal was a tough soldier, a loving husband and an affectionate family man. However, his bond with his battalion was the strongest. He thought of 1 Para as his family. This comes to the fore each time Mrs Birender Kaur Dyal talks about her late husband, a smile playing on her lips.

She never takes his name, referring to him only as *yeh* or *woh*, her voice soft and soaked with affection. In the last years of his life, cancer had seeped into Gen Dyal's body, weakening his vertebral column and racking his body with pain but Mrs Dyal says he was always supportive and smiling; a pillar of strength for her. He would encourage her to go for golf and call to check on her if she got late coming back home. She remembers only one occasion when, talking about his battalion and his friends whom he loved with all his heart, he told her quietly, "'*Jab main nahin hounga tab bhi yeh log tujhe itna hi pyar denge. Meri kami mehsus nahin hone denge* (When I won't be here, these people will give you just as much love even then.

They won't let you feel my absence)." He was right,' she says, her eyes bright. 'I get so much affection from his friends, his battalion, that they have become my own family; they are there for me at every step. *Par unki kami toh mehsus hoti hi hai* (But I do miss him),' she says.

When 1 Para celebrated its 250th Raising Day in 2011, Gen Dyal was quite unwell but he insisted on attending. The soldier who had scaled the heights of Sank and Sar and led the attack on Haji Pir could barely walk; he was in extreme pain, but even then, he stood up to give a speech. Three months later, cancer claimed him.

He is survived by his wife and daughter, Parveen, whom he used to dote on. They live in a beautiful house in Panchkula where one of the rooms bears the nameplate 'Haji Pir'. Memories of the rainy August day when the brave paratroopers of 1 Para scaled the pass with their rifles on their shoulders linger on.

The Battle of Asal Uttar

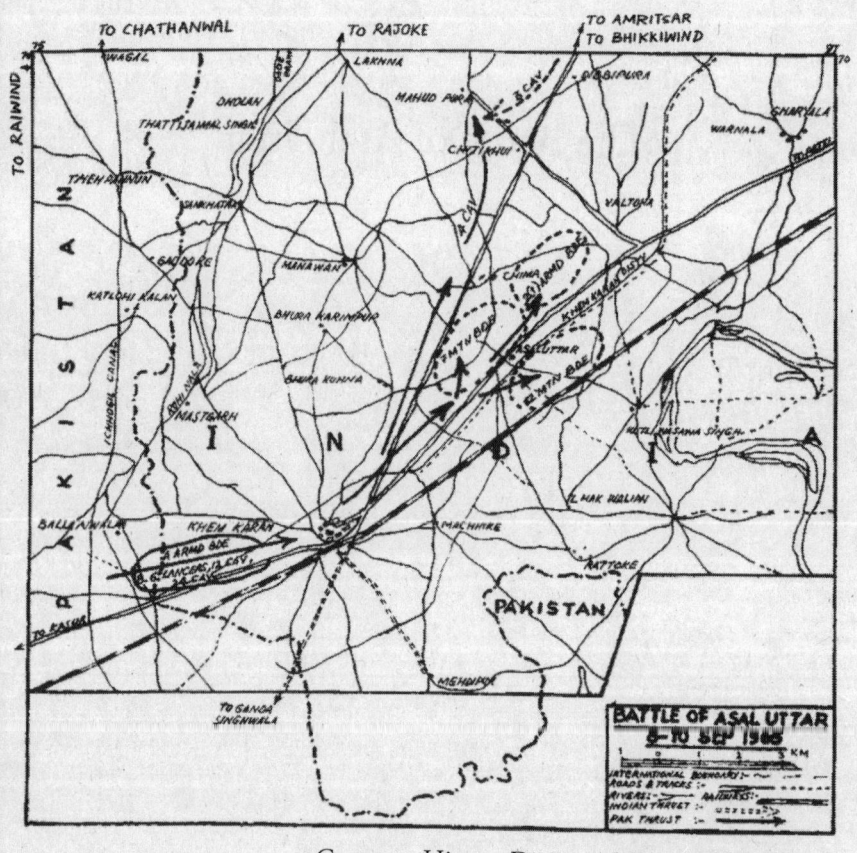

Courtesy: History Division, Ministry of Defence

On the morning of 1 September 1965, the nation woke up to a startling announcement on All India Radio. 'Pakistan has launched a massive attack with tanks and heavy artillery in the Chamb sector of Jammu and Kashmir. The enemy's objective seems to be the strategic Akhnoor Bridge. Prime Minister Lal Bahadur Shastri has declared that Pakistan will be given a fitting reply by the Indian Army,' it said.

The Prime Minister's statement was later described by Lt Gen Harbaksh Singh (Retd), VrC, then General Officer Commanding-in-Chief (GOC-in-C), Western Command, as 'the tallest of decisions taken by one of the shortest of men'. The general outline of the 'fitting reply' that Lt Gen Harbaksh Singh drew up had the Indian Army holding ground as close to the International Border as possible in the Punjab–Rajasthan sector and destroying any enemy that crossed over. He also planned on crossing the International Border and acquiring a large chunk of enemy territory which would give India a bargaining lever in the political talks that would be inevitable after the war was over. Part of this plan was the capture of Ichhogil Canal, a formidable water obstacle 140 ft wide and 15 ft deep, which Pakistan had built mainly for the defence of Lahore. The General intended to turn the tables by capturing the canal and using it as an Indian defence.

Pakistan had crossed the International Border in Jammu and Kashmir and was attacking Indian troops in the Chamb sector with two regiments of Patton tanks. However, they planned their main thrust from Kasur in the Lahore sector, from where they wanted to enter Punjab along the central line down the Road Khem Karan–Bhikhiwind and capture territory right up to the Beas River, and then pressurize India into giving up Kashmir. Maps confiscated later from vehicles of senior officers showed markings right up to Delhi. It is believed that in all their regiments, Pakistan had put up big posters of a Patton tank with the slogan 'March Up to Delhi'.

Having received ten regiments of Patton tanks from America, Pakistan felt confident of their strength against the Indian Armoured Corps which had only three regiments of Centurion tanks in addition to Shermans, some of which were World War II vintage and not even equipped with proper anti-tank guns. This led Pakistan to believe that they could easily press into India. They had not, however, taken into account the courage and resolve of Indian soldiers.

Three of the main units that bravely defended India on this axis were the Infantry battalion 4 Grenadiers and the armoured regiments 9 Horse and 3 Cavalry. This is their story, as told by Lt Col Hari Ram Janu (Retd), SM, of 4 Grenadiers; Lt Gen Jimmy Vohra (Retd), PVSM, SM, of 9 Horse; and Lt Col Ram Prakash Joshi of 3 Cavalry. The tank fight has been related by seventy-seven-year-old

Ris Maj (Hon Capt) Daya Chand Rathi (Retd), SM, of 3 Cavalry.

4 Grenadiers

It was 2 September 1965 when Fighting Fourth, the 4th Battalion of the Grenadiers, received orders to move for operations to the Khem Karan sector in Punjab. Their first task was to capture Theh Pannu Bridge on Ichhogil Canal.

The troops of 4 Grenadiers were located at Ambala cantonment where they had been moved from the eastern sector after suffering heavy casualties in the 1962 war. They had re-equipped and undergone mountain training, and had been on twenty-four-hour notice to move. When the orders finally came, the men were raring to go. Their defences were based on coordinated anti-tank and medium machine-gun arcs of fire. Sub Mool Chand, officiating anti-tank Platoon Commander, and his 106-mm recoilless (RCL) guns were to play a key role in the bitter battle that would rage for three days.

When I trace survivors from the battle, it is March 2015

Wheat is ripening in the fields—a dazzling sea of gold—and, from my window seat in the Shatabdi Express that is chugging its way to Jaipur, I can see women in fluorescent saris hard at work, cutting and stacking it up in neat piles. I'm on my way to meet Lt Col Hari Ram Janu (Retd), SM, of 4 Grenadiers. We spend the day in his Ambabari house where the seventy-two-year-old retired Colonel sifts through his memories and old black-and-white photographs of the war, and nostalgically remembers comrades lost and those still living. It was fifty years ago that he and his men fought the Battle of Asal Uttar, he says with a faraway look in his eyes. And then, in a conversation that stretches across a few hours, broken only by a traditional Rajasthani lunch, he tells me the unbelievable story of a battle where foot soldiers took on the mighty Patton tanks that America had so famously bragged could not be destroyed by anything in the world. 'We proved them wrong,' the septuagenarian chuckles softly, showing me a crumbling old photograph where he stands atop a captured Patton, arms akimbo.

6 September 1965

It is a warm September afternoon when the Grenadiers reach Dibbipura, one of the last towns on the Indo-Pak border. Lush sugar cane fields interspersed with ripening cotton stretch for miles around them. Where the International Border separates India from Pakistan, however, the land is barren. All that they can see is sarkanda or elephant grass growing wild all the way to Ichhogil Canal that roughly marks Pakistan's boundary.

Twenty-two-year-old Lt Hari Ram Janu is wading through chest-deep water, his .303 rifle held above his head as he trudges through the sarkanda that lashes his slush-caked body. Around him are 600 soldiers of his battalion, each at a distance of about 5.5 metres from the other, each holding his weapon high, ensuring that the water does not touch the ammunition packs strapped to their bodies. Artillery shells whistle past, quickening their heartbeat and triggering a buzz in their ears; above their heads, enemy bullets fly relentlessly. Pakistani soldiers have spotted them from the other side of Ichhogil and opened the gates of the canal, flooding the area completely. Undeterred by the water soaking them to the bone, and ignoring the bullets, the men trudge on.

The unit has been tasked to cross the International Border and capture the strategically located Theh Pannu Bridge on Ichhogil Canal. The attack was supposed to have been launched at 7 a.m. from Dibbipura but has been delayed owing to the late arrival of the troops who are able to reach the spot from Ambala only by 8 a.m. A and B companies of Jats are spearheading the daring daylight attack with C and D companies (Muslims and Dogras respectively) in direct support. Amongst the soldiers is CQMH Abdul Hamid who will bring laurels to the unit a few days later, but as of now he is just one of the many brave soldiers who are stoically putting their lives at risk to teach Pakistan a lesson it will not forget.

When the men reach the canal, they are surprised to find it heavily defended. While Pakistan has craftily lowered the bank of the canal on the Indian side, on their own bank they have constructed solid cement pillboxes with holes through which they keep watch and fire their weapons. 'There was a real din all around. Heavy machine-gun fire and artillery shelling from the enemy was coming straight at us, but luckily it was all passing overhead. I think God was with us. We suffered lightly with only four jawans injured and no fatal casualties,' Col Janu says as he recounts the storming of Theh Pannu Bridge. 'The flooding of the area by the Pakistanis also proved to be a boon for us as their artillery shells would land in the water, being rendered completely ineffective.'

Tired and soaking wet, the soldiers attack the bridge, braving the onslaught of the machine-gun fire. Their lightning advance across the border has worked to their advantage and by 10 a.m. they capture their objective. They are under heavy enemy fire throughout the day but face it stoically. Respite comes only at night. But that is when they learn that they are the only ones who have been able to capture their objective and are now completely exposed to the enemy on both sides. They also learn that 1 Armoured Division of the enemy is heading for the Khem Karan sector with the intention of capturing the Harike and Beas bridges and then Amritsar. The 4th Battalion is told to withdraw the next day and concentrate on building defences around the village of Asal Uttar so that Pakistan is not able to advance on the Khem Karan–Amritsar road.

Lt Janu is told to launch covering medium machine-gun fire as the troops withdraw. By 11 a.m. on 7 September the withdrawal is complete; Sub Daryao Singh of A coy is the last man to pass through the heavy enemy shelling. He is hit by a splinter that cuts into his chest and he falls, pleading with Lt Janu to leave him behind and move on. The young Lieutenant pulls him into a nearby nullah, gives him some water and inspects his wound (which is not fatal, he finds). The two then make their way back slowly, reporting to the Commanding Officer that the withdrawal is complete without any fatal casualties.

THE BATTLE OF ASAL UTTAR

The soldiers walk 4 km in their wet uniforms to reach Dibbipura where they halt for food. They then walk another 7 km to reach Chima village, the area they are to defend. Darkness is falling when the tired and sleep-deprived men start digging trenches and covering them with sugar cane stalks plucked from the fields so that they are not visible to enemy planes. It has been three days since they have changed their clothes, and the stink and grime of the water through which they have trudged cling to their sunburned and wind-lashed skin. They spend another anxious night in their shallow trenches, flitting in and out of sleep. News is rife that Pakistan will attack the next day. They have no idea that this is where they will take on the might of 1 Armoured Division of Pakistan in a three-day bloody battle that will be remembered in military history as the Battle of Asal Uttar. That it is fought in the village of Asal Uttar (which means 'befitting reply' in Hindi) is a coincidence that would not be lost on the soldiers.

'Chima, Asal Uttar, Khem Karan and Dibbipura were like ghost towns when we reached,' remembers Col Janu. 'The civil administration had been asked to get them cleared to minimize war casualties and the farmers had been told to move to camps set up around Amritsar. Most of the houses were locked and deserted; there were no children or animals around and the silence could be cut with a knife.'

Later, Lt Gen Jimmy Vohra of 9 Horse also tells me how they would watch from their Sherman tanks as rows of bullock carts would pass them by carrying men, women and children to safety at dusk.

On the ground

The soldiers of 4 Grenadiers were to defend the area between the villages of Asal Uttar and Chima, and they set up their posts on both sides of the road to Khem Karan from where the Pakistani tanks were expected to attack.

On the morning of 8 September, the men heard a deep rumble that warned them of approaching enemy tanks. The thick vegetation that hid them also obstructed their view of the road. In a while, however, soldiers manning the light machine-gun post raised a warning that they could see two tanks coming down the road. CQMH Hamid from C Company was on his recoilless gun, less than 30 metres from the road, his jeep hidden amidst the cotton crop. As the first tank came within shooting range, he fired, setting the tank ablaze. 'We were surprised to see the crew of two more tanks that were following, abandon their tanks and flee,' says Col Janu. 'We then realized that the Pakistanis fear being burned alive since their religion says that makes them kafirs.' At 11.30 a.m. came the second attack. This time, two troops of tanks (three in each troop) launched an attack—one against C Company, commanded by Lt Janu, and the other against B Company, commanded by Capt Kartar Singh, which was positioned to the right of the road. Hamid again shot one tank, his second that day, and the crew of the other two tanks abandoned them and fled. The troop against B coy withdrew. At about 2.30 p.m. came the third attack, this time against the B coy position. L/Nk Preet Singh, and Grenadiers Sukhpal, Jairam and Sriram destroyed two of the tanks while the third was abandoned by its crew. Thereafter the day passed peacefully, interrupted only by sporadic artillery fire from the enemy. The Grenadiers were upbeat. Nine tanks stood before them; four destroyed by recoilless-gun fire and five abandoned.

That afternoon, the two Company Commanders started making frantic requests for mines and Adjutant Capt Surender Chowdhary managed to get an engineer company to come around with anti-tank and anti-personnel mines. The engineers started around 7 p.m. and worked through the night, laying these out in front of the area held by the 4 Grenadiers companies. By 6 a.m. the next day, they completed their task and returned. The tired Grenadiers had hardly slept through the night and were trying to get some rest when, around 9 a.m., the silence of the morning was shattered by the sound of Sabre jets that started strafing the area. The men immediately took cover in their trenches. 'I was lying next to my trench, with a jerrycan under my head for a pillow, when I saw two Sabre jets pass right overhead. I instinctively rolled over into the trench. When the planes had passed, I found four bullet holes in the jerrycan that had been under my head. I was miraculously unharmed,' he recounts.

That day the Grenadiers face three tank attacks. The tanks come down the road in sets of three—at 9.30 a.m., 11.30 a.m. and finally at 2.30 p.m. Hamid destroys two tanks and Hav Bir Singh of B coy another two. Some of the anti-tank mines that had been laid the previous night are heard exploding and a few more tanks are disabled and deserted by the Pakistanis. The soldiers settle down for another night of fitful sleep. They know now that an entire Patton tank division of the Pakistan Army has been attacking them. However, they have faith in their World War II vintage recoilless rifles that have smashed, disabled and led to the abandonment of more tanks than an armoured formation could hope for in a tank-to-tank battle.

'Bade Imam mare gaye'

On 10 September, the day dawns bright but the Company Commanders are wary. They are expecting an Infantry attack. Every man is alert in his trench, finger on trigger. Nothing happens till 8.30 a.m., when they hear the rumble of enemy tanks again. Three Pattons are coming down the road—the first trundling down the middle, the other two following, one on either side. Hamid spots the first tank when it is 180-odd metres away, allows it to get closer and smashes it, quickly moving his jeep away so that its location is not picked up by the enemy. As had happened earlier, the soldiers in the remaining tanks flee. At 9 a.m. enemy shelling intensifies and many start landing in the C coy area, though nobody is injured. Soon the men spot another armoured attack. Hamid destroys his sixth tank. He spots the seventh tank at the same time that it spots him. There is no time to change position in the face of relentless artillery fire. Telling his driver and loader to get under cover, he aims his gun at the Patton even as it places him in its sight. Two simultaneous explosions rend the air—the tank as well as Hamid's jeep blow each other up simultaneously. The brave soldier is dead but there is no time to mourn as three enemy RCL jeeps from the Reconnaissance and Support Battalions come down the road. They are spotted by three intrepid Grenadiers—Shafiq, Naushad and Suleiman. Considered the bad boys of the battalion, they have nevertheless been given the responsibility of manning a light machine gun. Without waiting for firing orders, the three trigger-happy soldiers shoot down the crew of the first two jeeps, while the third manages to turn around and escape. A livid Lt Janu goes across to their post and gives them a stern dressing down, warning them not to fire till he orders them to do so. The three shake their heads remorsefully.

At 11 a.m. the enemy General Officer Commanding (GOC) approaches in a jeep driven by his Commander Artillery. Spotting his reconnaissance and supporting jeeps as well as his Regimental Commander's tank on the road (shot down by Hamid), he drives up to it, while his Rover jeep follows. As soon as he reaches the light machine-gun post, Grenadier Suleiman stands up in the trench. The GOC stops the jeep and calls out to the lonely Indian soldier, mistaking him for a straggler. When the soldier ignores his order, he steps out of the jeep and approaches the trench on foot, reaching for his pistol. By then the two other soldiers in the trench—Shafiq and Naushad—also stand up, pointing their weapons at him and look back wistfully at their Commander for orders to fire. Sensing the danger they are in, Lt Janu immediately shouts 'Fire,' and a volley of bullets hits the bewildered General who collapses on the spot. The Commander Artillery tries to turn the jeep and escape but he receives a burst of bullets on his forehead and slumps forward over the steering wheel. The Rover jeep manages to speed away but all its occupants except the driver are shot dead. A few minutes later a message being passed on the GOC's Rover is intercepted. It says, '*Bade Imam mare gaye* (The big boss has been killed).' The Pakistanis stop firing and an ominous stillness pervades the warm September afternoon.

Around 3 p.m., the rumbling of tanks is heard again. The Grenadiers count eight Patton tanks coming down the road, each with twenty armed men aboard it. Lt Janu takes it to be an Infantry attack and asks the Adjutant for 'Red over Red' (SOS fire on own position when enemy enters it). 'Our RCL gun had only one round of ammunition left; B Company had none; there was no way we could have taken on the mighty Pattons. So we duck into our trenches and ask our artillery to shell our own location,' he says. He hears the Pakistanis shouting, '*General sahab, hum aapko lene aaye hain* (General, we have come to get you).' The Pakistanis then spread out on both sides of the road and, picking up the bodies of their slain soldiers, place them on the tanks. Even as they are doing so, the Indian artillery guns come into action and, with a thundering noise, shells start pelting the area. The Pakistani tanks swiftly turn around and speed away. Once the shelling is over, the Grenadiers come out of their trenches and go around the area. They find the GOC's jeep with its star plates lying on the road, with the Commander's body still slumped over the wheel. It had probably gone unnoticed in the sudden panic created by the shelling. From the papers on his body, it is established that he is Brig A.R. Shamim, Commander Artillery Brigade of 1st Armoured Division of Pakistan. He is buried with full military honours at the Division headquarters. The GOC is later identified as Maj Gen Nasir Ahmed Khan.

Unsung heroes

Grenadiers Shafiq, Naushad and Suleiman were the bad boys of 4th Battalion who turned heroes in the war. They stand out not only in the history of 4 Grenadiers but also in that of all armies around the world as the only three foot soldiers who slew a General in battle. They never received any awards but what they did was remarkable.

No more attacks take place thereafter and the Battle of Asal Uttar is over. The regiment 4 Grenadiers is later awarded the Battle Honour Asal Uttar and the Theatre Honour Punjab. CQMH Abdul Hamid is decorated with the Param Vir Chakra and nine soldiers, including Lt Janu, are awarded the Sena Medal for their bravery in battle.

A visitor in white

Soon after ceasefire is declared on 21 September—the men of 4th Battalion are still located near Chima—Lt Janu is surprised to find some Pakistani soldiers approaching his location waving a white flag. With them is a lady in white who wants to meet him. Chairs are quickly pulled on to the road and a makeshift meeting place is created. With tears in her eyes, the visitor tells Lt Janu that she is the widow of the Commander Artillery who was shot down by his men. She requests him for the body of her husband. Lt Janu expresses his condolences but tells her that he is helpless as the body has already been handed over to the higher authorities. He tells her that her husband was a very brave soldier and assures her that he has been buried with full military honours as befitting an officer of his rank. All that he can offer her is a cup of tea. The lady accepts his offer graciously and the two share a quiet moment over tea, after which she is respectfully seen off by Lt Janu.

9 Horse

The 9 Horse was camping at Sangrur when war clouds started gathering; it was quickly moved to Ambala and made a part of 4 Mountain Division. Commandant Lt Col Arun Shridhar Vaidya (later Gen Vaidya, MVC [Bar], AVSM, Chief of Army Staff) was still living in a tent when marching orders came for his men. The fighting troops of 9 Horse had Sherman-IV tanks which they had received back in 1955. These tanks were equipped with a 75-mm anti-tank gun in a fully traversing turret which, though not enabling the crew to fire while on the move, allowed the gunner to aim while moving, so that the tank could fire fairly accurately as soon as it stopped.

When Pakistan attacked from the Khem Karan sector, 9 Horse was tasked with covering the troops of 62 and 7 Infantry Brigades and delaying the enemy for as long as possible. It was because of their dogged fight that Pakistan was not able to open the centreline and march into India through the Road Khem Karan–Bhikhiwind as they had planned. They were stopped in their tracks and forced to bypass and outflank, where they were intercepted by the Centurion tanks of 3 Cavalry and crushed completely.

This is the 9 Horse story as told by Lt Gen J.M. Vohra (Retd), PVSM, SM, who was a young Major commanding A Squadron during the war.

March 2015

Nearly half an hour early for my appointment with Lt Gen Jimmy Vohra, I am shown into his beautiful marble-floored Gurgaon house, tastefully done up with pale silk curtains and watercolours. The soothing strains of *gurbani* seep through the air and Mrs Vohra—tall, graceful and white-haired—walks in and keeps me company for a while. She tells me she was with her parents in Chandigarh when her husband went to war in 1965. She would frequently visit the families of the soldiers in Ambala, she says, assuring them that their men would come back safe. 'But, of course, everyone couldn't come back,' she says softly. 'We lost our boys; young girls lost their husbands—but then that's how wars are.'

Sharp at noon the General calls me to his first-floor study. Followed by his inquisitive Pekinese who is persistently yelping her disapproval at my presence, I climb the stairs that are fixed with a chairlift he uses to move up and down. He waits for me at the head of the stairs—wearing a white shirt and his regimental blue cravat—handsome and courteous, and leads me to a cosy sitting area. 'This is my den,' he says. 'My drinks are in the bar, my ice is in the fridge, my books are on the shelf.' And there, we time travel back to the sugar cane fields of Khem Karan, where the Sherman tanks of 9 Horse rolled down the Road Khem Karan–Bhikhiwind nearly fifty years ago. Khem Karan is a town on the Indo-Pak border, north of Ferozepur, on the western bank of the Beas.

3 September 1965
Ambala

It is a warm September night. Almost the entire regiment, including Commanding Officer Lt Col A.S. Vaidya, has gone to watch a movie at the regimental open-air theatre. Squadron Commander Maj Jimmy Vohra is sitting in the officers mess. Ever since 9 Horse has been moved suddenly from Sangrur to Ambala, and made a part of 4 Mountain Division, there has been perceivable tension in the air but Maj Vohra has no clue about the Indian Army's plans. The orders for him tonight are to stay near a phone. Around 9.30 p.m., the phone rings. The radio telephone operator is on the line. 'Your regiment should be ready to move tomorrow morning. Your first train is at 5 a.m., second at 8 a.m., third at . . .' he is rattling off, not bothering to answer any of the young Major's queries. Maj Vohra is initially shocked and then delighted. He has come to Ambala only to pick up his luggage as he has to go for a course at Ahmednagar. Instead, it seems like here is his chance to go to war. He informs the Adjutant; Lt Col Vaidya rushes to the regiment and orders are passed to start loading ammunition on to the tanks.

4 September 1965
Ambala

It is 6 a.m. and morning walkers on Staff Road are surprised to see as many as 14 Sherman tanks of A Squadron, 9 Horse, rolling down one after the other. Nobody knows where they are headed but the locals who are used to the sight shrug it off as yet another Army exercise. The tanks make their way to the railway station where they are quickly loaded on to a waiting train that immediately chugs off. Seated in a third-class compartment, Maj Vohra repeatedly requests the guard for a stop so that the men can cook a quick meal. They have been loading ammunition through the night and nobody has eaten, but his requests are ignored.

'It is only when the train stops to change the engine that the exasperated guard tells me the train's final destination. It is Makhu, a small town in Ferozepur district of Punjab, and there will be no halts in between. A jolt of thrill runs down my spine. Now I know for sure that we are going to war with Pakistan,' the General remembers.

Darkness has fallen by the time the train reaches Makhu. The men disperse into a thicket and, soon after, they start to cook. The next morning, the officers are called to Khem Karan guest house in civvies and addressed by the 62 Infantry Brigade Commander. The regiment 9 Horse is tasked with assisting 9 J&K Rifles in capturing a bandh on Rohi nullah.

The morning after, the tanks roll down to Khem Karan; this time the men are in uniform. They attack the bandh and capture it, taking the Pakistani rangers prisoner. The 9 J&K Rifles troops climb to the top of the bandh. The soldiers dig trenches and take up a defensive position there in case the enemy counter-attacks. Then the 9 Horse troops see their first death. They will later see hundreds of deaths and learn to take them in their stride. When the tanks come to harbour on the night of 6 September, they see villagers leaving their homes in bullock carts. News has reached the civilian population that Pakistan is going to attack and entire villages are being evacuated. The next day, the soldiers keep watch over the ghost villages as artillery shelling rips through the air and enemy aircraft fly overhead. At 4 p.m., 9 J&K Rifles is ordered to pull back, and 9 Horse shoots down two Pakistani Pattons that are coming towards them from the left and right. 'That was the first time we realized our Shermans could shoot down Pattons; it gave us a lot of confidence as we watched them go up in flames in front of us,' the General remembers, his eyes sparkling.

On 8 September, 9 Horse hides its tanks in the sugar cane fields and, as the Pakistani Pattons come within range, they shoot, often three guns blazing together to bring down a single Patton. They knock down eight of Pakistan's tanks and there is jubilation all around. At night, orders come to pull back after destroying the bridge on the Khem Karan distributary. The artillery unit 2 Field Regiment (Self-Propelled) asks for time since it has already dumped ammunition on the other side of the bridge. If left unspent, the enemy will use it. The move is stalled for a while and the artillery unit bombards Kasur Railway Station through the night, using it as a target to spend as much ammunition as possible. The guns are then brought back, the engineers blow up the bridge and, as the flames lick the air in the dark night, filling it with a deep orange glow, the soldiers and the Shermans make their way back to harbour.

The Shermans of 9 Horse A and B squadrons are tasked with blocking the path of the invading Pakistanis. When the Pakistani tanks roll down this way, they are forced to outflank from the main road. Here, the deadly Centurions of 3 Cavalry are waiting for them.

3 Cavalry

It is the evening of 1 September 1965. Ram Prakash Joshi (fondly called Jo in his regiment), Second Lieutenant of C Squadron, 3 Cavalry, is playing tennis in Ambala cantonment when he receives orders that all officers are to gather in the mess. Commandant Lt Col Salim Caleb (late Maj Gen Salim Caleb, MVC) soon reaches the officers mess and addresses his men.

He says, 'The Pakistanis have infiltrated into Jammu and Kashmir and our Prime Minister has asked the Indian Army to retaliate at the place and time of its own choosing.' The 3 Cavalry has been placed under the command of 2 Independent Armoured Brigade and tasked with countering tank threats from the enemy in the XI Corps area. XI Corps was responsible for the defence of Punjab. Lt Col Caleb tells them to prepare for a white-hot move, which means that trains carrying troops from Ambala cantonment will not be stopping anywhere before they reach their destination. A Squadron, under Maj Suresh Chander Vadera, is moved out the same night, while B Squadron, under Maj P.S. Belvalkar, and C Squadron, under Maj Narinder Singh Sandhu, are moved the next day. The troops and tanks (forty-five in all) disembark at Kadgil, near Jandiala Guru, one stop short of Amritsar.

When Pakistan attacks in the Khem Karan sector and tries to push back 4 Mountain Division, 3 Cavalry is tasked with defending Punjab's territory and destroying the enemy as it tries to advance. The regiment engages in tank battles with the Pattons of 1 Armoured Division of Pakistan. It faces four units of Pakistan in that operation—4 Cavalry, 24 Cavalry, 6 Cavalry and 5 Lancer. I hear the fascinating story of 3 Cavalry from septuagenarians Lt Col R.P. Joshi (Retd), who was a Second Lieutenant during the war, and Ris Maj (Hon Capt) Daya Chand Rathi (Retd), SM, who was gunner to C Squadron Commander Maj Sandhu.

March 2015

On cold winter nights seventy-seven-year-old Ris Maj (Hon Capt) Daya Chand Rathi (Retd), SM, sometimes wakes up from the throbbing pain in his bullet-scarred legs. Lying awake in the darkness, with his eyes shut, he often hears the rumbling of enemy tanks and the unmistakable fire of recoilless guns. His doctors call it Gunners Disease, but for him, those noises in his head are memory triggers that take him back to the village of Kalia Sangatra on the Indo-Pak border, where his company tanks faced action in the early days of September 1965. Fifty years flash past in the blink of an eye and he is twenty-seven once again. The sugar cane stalks are rustling in the wind, artillery shells are flying overhead and his dusty Centurion, along with two others, is waiting in the fields—hidden in the tall grass that can slice through skin as keenly as a knife.

I locate Ris Maj Daya Chand in the village of Lakhan Majra, 20 km from Rohtak, a three-hour drive from Delhi. Having lost his wife to cancer a few months back, and with no children of his own, Daya Chand lives alone. His brother's daughter-in-law cooks for him over a mud chulha and serves us sweet, milky tea and biscuits, smiling shyly from behind the bright red dupatta pulled low over her face. Daya Chand walks slowly and carefully, with a cane for support. His legs have practically frozen, he says; it has been fifty years since he shot down Pakistan's Pattons in the Battle of Asal Uttar but he delves into his memories effortlessly to tell me about the day three tanks of C Squadron, under Squadron Commander Maj Sandhu, faced action. 'We were ordered to go on the defensive about 10 km ahead of Chima village,' he says. 'I was gunner to Sandhu sahab. We had been told to stop Pakistan from advancing into our country. The orders from Commandant sahab were that till the last man was alive, not a single enemy tank should be allowed to go past.'

Maha Vir Chakra for Lt Col Caleb

On the night of 17 September 1965, All India Radio announced the award of a Maha Vir Chakra to Lt Col Salim Caleb for exercising his command with dauntless courage, calmness and fortitude and for inspiring his men to fight fearlessly. His citation mentions the tank battle on 10 September where fifteen enemy Patton tanks were destroyed and nine captured in working condition.

It was a fiery tank battle, he remembers; the tanks coming at them were too many to count. 'Swr Sahab Singh, the driver of our tank, was the first to spot them. He warned me that there was a Patton tank to our right. Sahab gave us orders to fire. I immediately fixed it in my gunsight, told my loader Ram Singh, "*Gun load kar de, bhai* (Load the gun)" and fired.' Daya Chand remembers that the time was around 2.30 p.m. when the first Patton tank went up in flames before their eyes. Right behind it was another one that was shot down as well. They managed to hit four tanks, one after the other, but Daya Chand admits he would be lying if he said he was not scared. 'The enemy tanks just kept coming one after the other. Nervously, I asked Swr Singh, "*Kitne honge, bhai?* (How many do you think there are?)" He shrugged without uttering a word and looked really worried.'

Just then another enemy tank emerged from amidst the sugar cane fields and that was hit too, he recalls. It was followed by two jeeps mounted with recoilless guns that were shot down as well. However, an anti-tank gunshot hit the Centurion and jammed its firing circuit. The crew quickly changed the fuse and managed to hit one more enemy tank but by then they had taken another hit. 'Our tank's idle broke; it tilted towards one side and clattered to a stop,' Daya Chand recounts. 'I could hear Major sahab ordering us to evacuate and take cover. He and the loader managed to climb out of the tank but as soon as driver Sahab Singh opened the hatch and tried to step out, he was hit by a burst of fire. *Hamari ankhon ke saamne gir pada aur wahin khatam ho gaya* (He collapsed in front of our eyes and died on the spot),' Daya Chand says softly.

'I was trying to get out when enemy machine-gun fire started hitting the tank like the monsoon rain and I went back in. When the firing finally stopped, I tried to come out once again but the cord of my pistol got caught in the tank and I hung there, trapped; a burst of machine-gun fire hit me in both my legs.' Daya Chand says he thought he would die but he did not. He eventually managed to get free and dragged himself up to where his comrades were waiting for him, sitting beside some women who were digging mud to plaster their houses. They saw the blood oozing out of his legs and the trail of crimson behind him. Until then, in the heat of the battle, he had not felt any pain. His wound was dressed with whatever field patties the men were carrying and all of them then half carried, half dragged him to their unit location 7 km away. Once there, Daya Chand fainted from the pain and loss of blood. He was shifted to PGI Chandigarh where an emergency surgery saved his legs as well as his life. His father came to see him a few days later, as he was drifting in and out of consciousness. 'Whenever people came to look me up, my father would tell them, *"Jab ladai se bach ke aa gayo te ab te bach hi jayego* (When he has come out of the war alive, he will survive this too),"' he says. Daya Chand came back to his battalion three months later; he was awarded a Sena Medal for his bravery and served until his retirement.

As the history of 3 Cavalry—based on which the rest of this battle has been recreated—reveals, the unit had been tasked with blocking the main routes of enemy advance. At 11 a.m. on 8 September their Centurions started moving southwards on the Road Khem Karan–Bhikhiwind. B Squadron led with Regimental Headquarters, and C Squadron—two troops short—following. A Squadron was to move along the Patti–Valtoha–Khem Karan road.

The leading elements of B Squadron, having reached south of Chima village, were the first to face action. It was 2.37 p.m. when gunner Charan Singh sighted what he described as a strange form that suddenly shaped into a Patton tank. With sure but sweaty fingers and a short prayer on his lips, he pressed the trigger. The enemy tank burst into flames. The first blow had been dealt. Within minutes, a second Patton tank was hit as well. The Patton tank's reputation of being invincible crumbled right there, raising the morale of the men.

C Squadron, under 2Lt Joshi, saw action on 9 September. Jo, now seventy-five, remembers how he and his five tanks were positioned near a nullah 5 km from Mastgarh, well hidden amidst the sugar cane. He was lying in wait under his tank, with his binoculars and walkie-talkie, when he heard his gunner Swr Mata Din call out, '*Sahab, dushman ke tank aa gaye hain* (Sir, the enemy tanks have arrived).'

'Since we were on higher ground, I could see an enemy tank heading in our direction. It must have been about 4 km away,' he says. He quickly summoned his men. 'I told them we were the fortunate ones who had got the opportunity to fight for our country, and quoted a few lines from the Gita to them,' he recounts. The men then got into their tanks, which had been camouflaged with sugar cane plucked from the fields, and waited for the enemy to come within firing range.

'Since we were very well camouflaged, I knew they could not see us, but the moment we fired our first shot we would give away our location. My boys were eager to take on the enemy but I warned them that no one would fire before my tank, we would just fix them in our gunsight,' Lt Col Joshi says. When the first tank came within shooting range, he told Swr Mata Din to fire. As soon as they saw the first tank go up in flames, the rest of the Centurions opened fire. Within six minutes, six of Pakistan's Patton tanks were up in flames. Lt Col Joshi says he initially thought there were only three tanks; then he realized there were six. They later found out that Pakistan had attacked with an entire regiment of forty-five tanks. The 3 Cavalry regimental history says that twelve tanks were destroyed in that operation. Lt Col Joshi doesn't put a figure to it but says that the tank battle lasted two and a half hours, from 4.30 p.m. to 7 p.m. 'As night fell, the area before us was like a Diwali *mela*—the tanks were burning, orange flames licking the sky, their ammunition was going up like rockets.'

When a victorious 2Lt Joshi walked back to the Regimental Headquarters later that night, he got an unexpected bear hug from his Commanding Officer who then ordered a drink for the young Major. 'It was a big moment for me. Lt Col Caleb was so strict that he had disciplined us by getting pleats stitched into our jeans,' he says with a chuckle.

On 10 September, it appeared that the enemy would launch a tank assault in the Mohamedpura area where A Squadron was deployed. Since the tanks were moving through the field amidst the tall stalks of sugar cane, it was going to be difficult for the men to distinguish enemy tanks from their own. Lt Col Caleb understood this only too well and his conversation with Squadron Commander Maj Vadera ended with a piece of hard advice: 'Anyone who remains cooler for longer under stress will win. Identify, take aim and then shoot well; God be with you.'

A Squadron watched and waited with bated breath. Around 5.30 p.m., Pattons were finally sighted. The Squadron Commander's gunner Swr Dhirpal Singh destroyed three Pattons roughly at the rate of one a minute. Two more Pattons were destroyed by Nb/Ris Jagdeo Singh's Centurion. The enemy tank assault petered down and finally came to a stop. At the end of that day's action, five enemy tanks lay damaged in the fields.

Thereafter, all Centurions were ordered to fire their main guns as well as machine guns to show the enemy that 3 Cavalry's defended position was held in strength. By then, the Centurions needed immediate replenishment of ammunition, and tank Commanders started asking for permission to withdraw in order to stock up. But Lt Col Caleb refused, saying, 'No one will change position or withdraw.' Instead, jeeps from the inter-communication troop were brought in to replenish ammunition.

Maj Vadera mounted an abandoned Patton tank (BA no. 77651), read up the manufacturer's instructions and, much to the delight of all present, managed to start it. The news of the capture was radioed to 4 Mountain Division and caused much jubilation all around.

GOC 4 Mountain Division Maj Gen Gurbaksh Singh visited the regiment to see for himself what he had heard and it was decided that the serviceable Patton would be driven into their own territory. It was decided that Maj Vadera would report when he started his move forward and drive that tank with its headlights on even in daylight. He was told that the main gun of the captured tank would point towards the enemy and the tank would fly a white flag. Since a white flag was not available, a white vest had to suffice. Fifteen minutes later, Pakistan's Patton tank BA no. 077651 turned up at the 3 Cavalry Regimental Headquarters proudly driven by Maj Vadera, the white 'flag' prominently in place. A thorough search later led to many more abandoned Patton tanks being discovered in the fields. Ris Jagat Singh, the officiating Risaldar Major, and 2Lt P.J.S. Mehta were ordered to immobilize them.

Since some members of the Pakistani tank crew were still seeking shelter in the sugar cane fields, it was feared that they might make an attempt to recover their abandoned tanks. To foil any such attempt, the banks of a nearby minor canal were broken, flooding the entire area. All India Radio broadcast the news of the capture of these Pattons in its afternoon bulletin. So many enemy tanks littered the area that Lt Col Caleb requested the Brigade Commander to arrange for numbering the enemy tanks with paint in order to make counting easier. All the turrets of the captured enemy tanks therefore showed a number in white paint in addition to their original Urdu serial numbers.

Later that evening, 3 Cavalry recovered another war trophy—operational order no. G-3548 (copy no. 3) of Pakistan's 4 Armoured Brigade, dated 8 September 1965. This clearly stated that 4 Armoured Brigade was to secure Beas Bridge on the main Grand Trunk Road. The order now hangs in the Regimental Officers' mess. Lt Col Caleb called it a 'colossal enemy dream come untrue'.

At 3.30 a.m. on 23 September 1965, the shelling finally stopped. A queer silence descended on the battlefield of Asal Uttar. Ceasefire had been imposed.

Patton Nagar: The graveyard of Pattons

The second Indo-Pak war was witness to the largest tank battle in military history between World War II and 1965. It is said that close to a thousand tanks on both sides took part in the deadly offensives.

One of the most fascinating war trophies of the Battle of Asal Uttar, which also means befitting reply, was the Bhikhiwind village of Khem Karan where battered and abandoned enemy tanks were lined up by the victorious Indian Army. According to *War Despatches*, a book written by Lt Gen Harbaksh Singh (Retd), VrC, who was Army Commander, Western Command, in 1965, in three days of the war, seventy-five Pakistani tanks were destroyed or abandoned. These included the entire tank fleet of 4 Cavalry, whose Commanding Officer, twelve officers and several soldiers of Other Ranks surrendered on the morning of 11 September. Tanks captured at the Battle of Asal Uttar by India's 4 Mountain Division were displayed here for some time after which they were shipped to various cantonments and army establishments in India to be put on display as war trophies. Though some reports peg the number of displayed tanks at sixty, Lt Col H.R. Janu of 4 Grenadiers says he had counted as many as 103 tanks after the battle. Local residents soon began to call this strip of land Patton Nagar. After the war, Films Division of India shot a documentary on the battlefield. Even as their cameras rolled, Corps of Electrical and Mechanical Engineers (EME)

> dragged battle-scarred enemy tanks to this point, which was also referred to as the Patton Tank Graveyard. Prime Minister Lal Bahadur Shastri too visited the site and remarked with pride, '*Maine toh apni zindagi mein itni tuti hui bail-gadiyan bhi nahin dekhin* (I haven't even seen as many wrecked bullock carts in my life).' Patton Nagar served as a unique memorial to all those who fought and fell at Asal Uttar or survived the ordeal of that battlefield to fight another day.

The people's war

It is remarkable that 9 Horse, 4 Grenadiers, 3 Cavalry and 21 Rajasthan Rifles successfully held back an entire armoured division (350 tanks) of Pakistan for seventy-two hours.

For the valour the battalion displayed on the battlefield, 4 Grenadiers was awarded nine Sena Medals (SM) (including one for Lt Col Janu), two Vishisht Seva Medals (VSM) and the Battle Honour Asal Uttar. CQMH Abdul Hamid was posthumously decorated with the Param Vir Chakra (PVC) the highest gallantry award of India. Military historian Steven Zaloga says that Pakistan admitted to losing 165 tanks during the 1965 war, more than half of which were knocked out during the Battle of Asal Uttar. A famous participant in the battle was Pervez Musharraf, who went on to become Army Chief of Staff and President of Pakistan. At the time, Musharraf was a young Lieutenant of artillery in the 16 (SP) Field Regiment, 1st Armoured Division Artillery.

Its back broken, the Pakistani Armoured Division eventually decided to pull out and go towards Sialkot, leaving troops behind in Khem Karan.

The 1965 war has rightly been called a people's war by Lt Gen Harbaksh Singh (Retd), VrC, in his book *War Despatches*. All the soldiers I interviewed agreed that many bravehearts of this war were not soldiers in uniform. They were the resilient people of Punjab. Young farmers would crawl right up to the soldiers through the enemy shelling, bringing humble yet priceless offerings of food—roti and sabzi wrapped in old muslin, steel buckets spilling over with buttermilk, rich kheer in tiffin boxes. They would generously contribute in whatever way they could to look after the fighting soldiers. Transporters would offer their trucks free of cost, boys would line up to load and unload ammunition, old sardars with flowing white beards would blatantly refuse to leave their homes, telling the soldiers they preferred to die where they were born. They would pull their charpoys out in the sun and watch the battle unfolding before them like a television show, completely unmindful of their own safety.

. . .

CQMH ABDUL HAMID has knocked down six enemy
tanks, constantly changing his position to keep his RCL
jeep camouflaged amidst the tall cotton crop. Another
tank is lumbering towards him, but he does not have time
to move as it has spotted him. Both place each other
in their gunsight and shoot. At the same moment that
the tank is blown up, its shell hits Hamid's jeep.
There is a loud blast, fire and smoke, and then there
is complete silence.

CQMH Abdul Hamid

Param Vir Chakra

In a modest house near Dullahpur Railway Station, about 4 km from a town called Dhamupur in Ghazipur district of Uttar Pradesh, lives a frail old woman in her eighties. She has almost lost her hearing. Small and shrunken, with a faded dupatta covering her head, she could easily get lost in a crowd. Yet she needs to be remembered, particularly by those of us who live in a free India and have our families around us, because she is one of the many who paid a big price for the freedom that we enjoy today.

For Rasoolan Bibi, wife of late Company Quarter Master Havildar Abdul Hamid, PVC, it will be exactly fifty years since her husband walked out of the house with his green canvas holdall on his back, never to return. The year was 1965. The month August. Dullahpur Railway Station, from where her grandson Jameel Alam catches a train to Varanasi almost every morning to go to work, is where CQMH Hamid too had caught the local train to Varanasi that night. He was

on his way to Punjab, where his battalion—4 Grenadiers—
was deployed in the Khem Karan sector. It was a dark night
preceded by a string of bad omens, and Rasoolan had tried
her best to make her husband postpone his journey. '*Par
unhone hamar ek na suni. Hans kar bole fauj bulayi hai, janohi
parego* (But he did not listen to me. He said with a smile
that the Army has called me, I will have to go).' For Hamid,
she says—with a hint of pride even in her sadness—the Army
always came first.

There is a glint of tears in Rasoolan's eyes as she watches her
husband pack that day. He is going to war for the second
time. Hamid has been studiously ignoring her. He folds his
cotton mattress and places it in his holdall, turning the edges
in to make it fit. He also shoves in a pillow and two single
bed sheets, neatly folded by Rasoolan. Then he packs his
uniforms and shoes, and a muffler that she had bought for
him from a fair in a nearby village sometime back. Just as he
rolls up the bedding, pressing it down with one knee to pack
it tighter, the belt holding it together snaps under the strain,
leaving one half hanging limply from his hand.

'It is a bad omen, you should not go today,' Rasoolan
points out, the tears spilling over now. Hamid turns to her
with a gentle smile. 'I can't do it,' he says. 'I have orders to
join the battalion. But don't worry about me, I will be fine.
Don't forget that I had come back safe from the '62 war also.'
He gets on with his packing, asking her to fetch him a rope
instead.

The so-called bad omens continued that evening, says Jameel Alam. Just as Hamid is leaving the house accompanied by neighbours and relatives, with his best friend Baccha Singh pulling along a bicycle on which his black trunk has been loaded, the chain of the cycle breaks. Someone in the small crowd points out that it is not a good sign, but he just shrugs it off. When they reach the railway station and find that his train has already left, Baccha tells him it seems as if Allah does not want him to go. 'Stay back tonight, take another train tomorrow,' he tries to reason, but Hamid is determined to go. He politely tells them to return; he will wait for the next train. With that he sets his trunk down on the platform and sits astride it. He has made his decision. His friends and family go back reluctantly, wishing him a safe journey. That is the last they see of him.

A disciplined soldier

Lt Col Janu (Retd), SM, Hamid's Company Commander during the 1965 war, remembers him as a simple, straightforward man who didn't speak much. 'He was honest and sincere, and had completed his recoilless (RCL) gun training from Mhow. He had done very well, scoring an instructor grading,' he says. When 4 Grenadiers got orders to move for war, Hamid had also been recalled from his leave like all the others and had joined the battalion as quickly as he could. 'Since he was RCL-qualified and we were short of men, he was removed from quarter master duties (looking after stores and provisions) just a few days before the war and put on the RCL gun.'

Before he joined the Army, Hamid had been a tailor. He would sit with a sewing machine in his house in Dhamupur, stitching clothes for people, with the chatter of his kids echoing around him. No one could have guessed then that he would become a lethal tank slayer who would single-handedly make such a big difference to the outcome of the war. Col Janu acknowledges this with a smile. 'Before they join the Army, some of our men are dhobis, some are tailors; but after their military training, they are all soldiers, and Hamid was one of our bravest,' he says.

8 September, Khem Karan sector
9 a.m.

CQMH Abdul Hamid sits in the co-driver's seat of his jeep which has a recoilless gun mounted on it, and as he passes through the sugar cane fields, he can hear the rustling wind in his ears. The jeep trundles over a narrow mud track ahead of Chima village. He knows Pakistan had launched an attack with a regiment of Patton tanks and has barged right into the forward position. He hears the rumble of armour first and then catches sight of a few Pakistani Patton tanks that are heading in the direction of his battalion. Taking cover behind the tall crop, he points his gun in their direction and waits. The Grenadiers hold their fire so as not to warn the enemy. Just as the tanks come within shooting distance, Hamid asks his loader to load the gun and fire. He watches the shell as it shoots out and arches towards the first enemy tank. Even as he picks up his binoculars, he hears the blast. The tank goes up in flames in front of his eyes. Hamid and his men rejoice. '*Shabaash!* (Bravo!)' he mouths and they exchange wide smiles. They spot the crew of the two following tanks dismount and flee. He orders the jeep driver to reverse and move.

Around 11.30 a.m., the battalion is subjected to heavy artillery shelling. Soon after, they hear the familiar rumble again. Hamid whips out his binoculars. Three more tanks are heading in their direction. He asks his driver Mohammad Naseem to position his jeep in the middle of the field so that it is hidden from view and, adjusting his weapon, he waits. The moment the tank comes within shooting distance, he signals to the loader and watches the trajectory of the shell. It hits its target and one more tank is aflame in front of his eyes, while the remaining two are again abandoned by the Pakistanis. By the end of the day, Hamid has destroyed two tanks, while four have been abandoned. They call on the engineers to immediately lay out anti-tank mines in the area as that is where the enemy tanks are coming from. They do the best they can in the little time available. It is clear that the battalion is facing a Brigade-level attack from the Pakistani armoured forces and all they have to fight them with are recoilless guns. That doesn't daunt the soldiers who are in high spirits after their initial victories.

The next morning Hamid is back at his recoilless gun. The battalion also faces an air attack from Pakistani Sabre jets but these don't do much damage. By the end of the day, he and his team have shot down two more tanks—a remarkable achievement. That night Hamid sleeps peacefully. His citation, crediting him with the destruction of four tanks, has been sent for the award of Param Vir Chakra. The following day he shows up on the battlefield yet again, to destroy as many as three more tanks; however, these will not enter his records as his citation has already been sent.

On 10 September, 4 Grenadiers comes under heavy enemy shelling. After that there is another assault by enemy tanks. They are moving in a formation of three. Hamid lies in wait, hidden by the thick vegetation and, when the first tank gets close, he blows it up, quickly asking his driver Naseem to move away. Just as they do, a tank shell bursts at the very spot where they were a few minutes back. By then the brave Grenadiers have moved to another point behind a thicket of babool trees, from where they are training their gun on another Patton. They shoot down one more Patton. By now, the shelling has started. The tanks have noticed the RCL jeeps and they start raining down concentrated machine-gun fire on them. Hamid is tricking them by constantly changing his position and keeping his jeep camouflaged amidst the tall cotton crop growing in the fields. Another tank is slowly lumbering towards him and he does not have time to move since they have both spotted each other. He tells his driver and loader to jump off. '*Hum kapas ke khet mein kude aur roll hokar nale mein ludak gaye* (We jumped into the cotton field and rolled into a drain),' says Naseem. Both Hamid and the enemy tank place each other in their sights and shoot. Both shells hit their targets. There is a loud blast, fire and smoke. At the same moment that the tank is blown up, its shell hits the RCL jeep. Hamid doesn't get time to jump off. A deafening blast follows and then there is complete silence. CQMH Hamid is dead. He has destroyed a total of seven enemy tanks, many more than what an armoured formation could take on.

For his remarkable achievement, bravery and courage, CQMH Abdul Hamid is awarded the Param Vir Chakra posthumously. The battalion is awarded the Battle Honour Asal Uttar and the Theatre Honour Punjab. It is a first in military history that a battalion armed with nothing more than recoilless guns has fought off an armoured division.

Abdul Hamid was born on 1 July 1933 in Dhamupur village of Uttar Pradesh's Ghazipur district. His family house still stands there—quiet and crumbling—in the midst of golden wheat fields. No one lives there now, but there was a time when the house would reverberate with the tinkle of laughter and the whirring of the sewing machine. Hamid's father, Mohammad Usman, was a tailor and Hamid would help him with the cutting and stitching whenever he could. His mother, Sakina Begum, had her hands full with six children—four boys, including Hamid, and two girls. As a boy, Hamid attended Basic Primary School, Dhamupur, and passed the eighth standard from Junior High School, Deva. He was nature's child and, right from the beginning, enjoyed sports like wrestling, swimming, hunting and *gatka* or sword fighting. His grandfather had an *akhada* where Hamid would take wrestling lessons and participate in occasional bouts. At the age of fourteen, he was married to Rasoolan Bibi and they had five children—a daughter and four sons.

Hamid was always a proud man. His grandson Jameel recounts an incident that throws light on this facet of Hamid's personality. Haseen Ahmed, the zamindar of a nearby village who was a good marksman, offered a large cash reward to anyone who could shoot down a rare bird after his own attempts proved unsuccessful. Hamid borrowed his friend Baccha's gun and shot the bird, but refused to go to the zamindar to ask for the prize money. Baccha went there instead and when the zamindar asked for Hamid to come to collect the prize, he refused saying, 'I might be poor, but I don't go begging to people's houses.' Finally the zamindar had the prize money sent to Hamid.

He was twenty years old when a recruitment camp was held in Ghazipur. He dropped his scissors and sewing machine and rushed there. He was six feet two inches tall, a fine wrestler and marksman, and was immediately selected. He was recruited into the Army at the Varanasi branch recruitment office. After undergoing his training at the Grenadiers Regimental Centre at Nasirabad, he was posted to 4 Grenadiers in 1955. Initially, he served in a rifle company and was then posted to a Recoilless Platoon. He fought in the 1962 war in Thang La, then North East Frontier Province, as a part of 7 Mountain Brigade, 4 Mountain Division, and came back disappointed with the war. After ceasefire was declared, his unit moved to Ambala where Hamid was appointed Company Quarter Master Havildar (CQMH) of an administration company. When Pakistan attacked in the Rann of Kutch in April 1965, 4 Grenadiers was ordered to move forward and collect their 106 recoilless guns from the nearest ordnance depot. Hamid was one of the non-commissioned instructors. In the absence of anti-tank detachment commanders, he was told to take over an anti-tank detachment. He was an astute marksman and an expert anti-tank gunner; with a new anti-tank gun at his disposal, he made a substantial difference to the outcome of the war. He died on 10 September 1965.

Rasoolan Bibi had been worried ever since her husband went to war. She would go about her household chores as usual, but her mind would wander in the sugar cane fields of Punjab. Since she didn't know exactly where her husband had been sent to fight, she would wonder where he could be and pray for his safe return. She had been listening to the radio that morning when she heard the news that a fearless soldier from 4 Grenadiers had been killed in the Battle of Asal Uttar after destroying four Pakistani tanks. It was CQMH Abdul Hamid. He was awarded the Param Vir Chakra, the country's highest gallantry award. '*Dukh bahut bhayan lekin hum itna soch leenhi, hamar aadmi chali geeni par kitna naam kar geeni* (I was grief-stricken, but then I told myself, my man had died but he had made such a name for himself),' says the old lady. The Param Vir Chakra was handed over to Rasoolan Bibi by President Sarvepalli Radhakrishnan at the Republic Day parade of 1966.

There are only two things that Ghazipur is famous for, quips Jameel—the opium factory and his grandfather. 'Class six students read about Vir Abdul Hamid in their Hindi literature books,' he tells me. When he was in school, he had read it too. '*Hume bahut garv hota tha ki woh hamare dadaji thhe. Dadaji toh nahin rahe, par aaj bhi bacche unke bare mein padhte hain. Yeh koi choti baat nahin* (I used to feel very proud that he was my grandfather. Grandfather is no longer with us, but even today children read about him. That is no small matter),' he says. A half smile plays on his lips. It is the same smile we see on Hamid's face when he looks at us from postage stamps and from posters put up in Army cantonments.

Footnote

There is ambiguity about the number of tanks Hamid destroyed. According to *War Despatches* by Lt Gen Harbaksh Singh, who was Army Commander, Western Command, during the 1965 war, Hamid spotted four tanks in a sugar cane field coming towards his company. Hiding his jeep behind a mound, he shot three of them at point-blank range. He also managed to hit the fourth but was blown to bits when a 90-mm shell struck his jeep. However, Hamid's Company Commander Col Janu puts the number of destroyed tanks at seven. It is believed that since CQMH Abdul Hamid's citation for Param Vir Chakra had been sent on 9 September, the three tanks that he destroyed a day later did not find a place in the records.

The Battle of Phillora

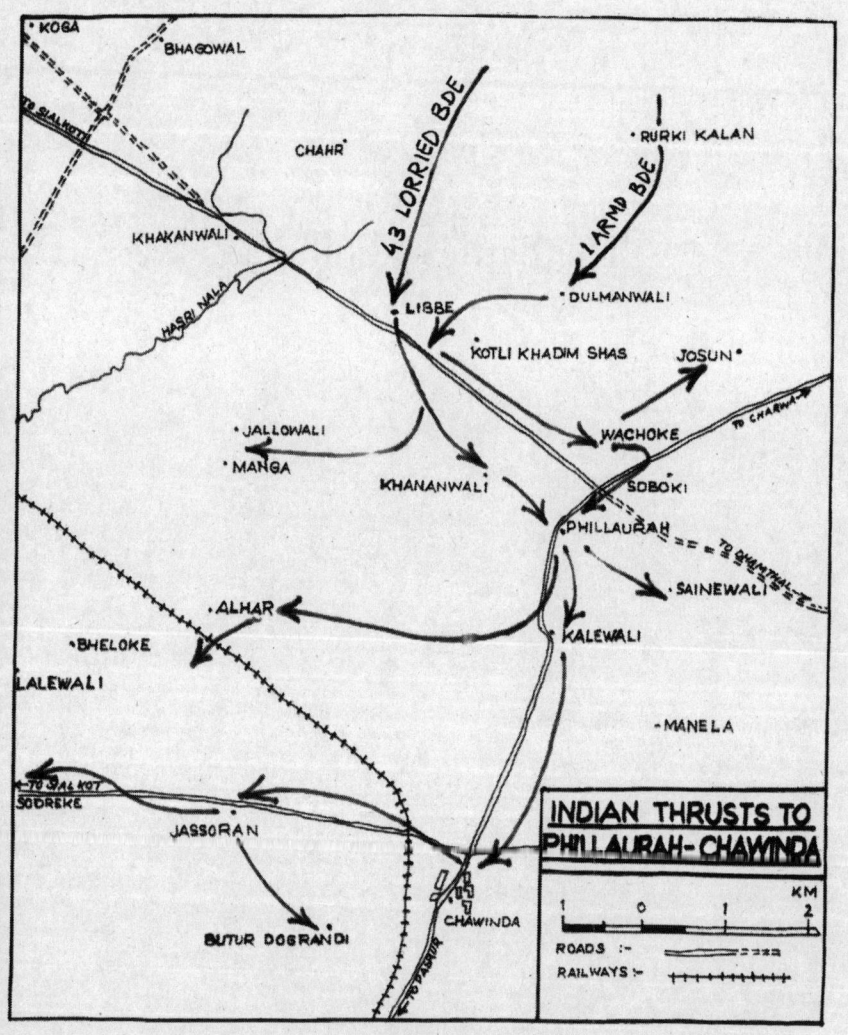

Courtesy: History Division, Ministry of Defence

In 1947, at the time of the partition of India, six armoured regiments were given to Pakistan and twelve to India. By 1965 both nations had equal numbers, with seventeen armoured regiments each. However, the then Prime Minister Jawaharlal Nehru's policy of non-alignment led to America wooing Pakistan which was only too happy to receive both financial and military aid from them. The result was that the Pakistan Army gained technical superiority while the Indian Army continued to function mostly with World War II vintage weapons and equipment. The difference was apparent in the armoured regiments too. Only four regiments of the Indian Army had Centurions, while most others had Sherman tanks which were no match for the American Pattons and Chaffees. Pakistan also had much better aircraft and state-of-the-art M47 and M48 guns. They had airburst fuses which did not rupture on impact but exploded 45 metres above the ground, causing greater damage. But what the Indian soldiers lacked in terms of equipment, they made up for in sheer grit, turning the tables on Pakistan. The Battle of Phillora illustrates this perfectly.

One of the fiercest tank battles of the 1965 war, it was the first major engagement between the two warring nations in the Sialkot sector and coincided with the Battle of Asal Uttar, where the Pakistan armoured regiments suffered heavily. The battle started on 8 September, when Indian troops crossed the border and launched a massive attack in the Phillora sector. India's 1st Armoured Division was on the offensive in the area with three brigades—1st Armoured Brigade, 43 Lorried Infantry Brigade and 1 Artillery Brigade—and four armoured regiments—4 Horse (Hodson's Horse), 17 Horse (Poona Horse), 16 Cavalry and 2 Lancers. They faced stiff opposition from Pakistan's 6th Armoured Division. The Pakistanis also made air attacks but these inflicted little damage on the tank columns, though the lorry and Infantry columns suffered. After one day of intense fighting, the beaten Pakistani troops made a tactical retreat towards Chawinda, where the last battle was fought before ceasefire was declared. In the Battle of Phillora, 1st Armoured Division destroyed fifty-one enemy tanks—of which 4 Horse destroyed twenty-seven—but in the process, it lost six tanks, with damages to nine more.

September 1965, Army Base Hospital, Delhi

The war of 1965 is over. A Sikh soldier is lying on his hospital bed, almost completely covered in blood. He is so severely burned that his wounds cannot be bandaged. He is waiting for Prime Minister Lal Bahadur Shastri to come up to him. The Prime Minister is walking from bed to bed, visibly anguished by the suffering of the brave soldiers—amputees, landmine victims, and those injured in shelling and bayonet attacks. When he reaches the Sikh officer, he pats his head affectionately and sees tears in his eyes. 'Major, you belong to one of the finest armies in the world. This doesn't behove you,' the Prime Minister tells him. The Major, who can barely speak because of the intense pain he is in, replies, 'Sir, I'm not pained because of any injury. I'm anguished that a soldier is not being able to salute his Prime Minister.' A deeply touched Lal Bahadur Shastri goes on to quote the officer's reply many times in public gatherings. The officer succumbs to his injuries a few days later. He is Maj Bhupinder Singh, MVC, Bravo Squadron, 4 Horse, the armoured regiment that is credited with destroying twenty-seven enemy tanks in Phillora. On 19 September in the Battle of Sodreke, Maj Singh's tank was hit by an enemy Cobra missile and caught fire. It had destroyed four enemy tanks by then. While the driver died on the spot, Maj Singh and his gunner Swr Vir Singh suffered grievous burns. Swr Vir Singh survived, while Maj Singh couldn't.

June 2015

With dark, piercing eyes, a flowing beard and a proud moustache, Dfr Vir Singh of Bravo Company, 4 Horse, has an arresting presence. He is seventy-eight years old and lives in Chingar Kalan village of Dasua tehsil, Hoshiarpur district. In the summer months, he says, his skin crawls. In winter, it feels as if a thousand needles are pricking his body. Painful memories of the war have stayed with him these fifty years. He was so badly burned, he says, that his face was unrecognizable and most of his fingers had twisted backwards. For four months he was completely blind and regained his eyesight in a slow and painful process. The missile that had ripped his tank apart had even melted some of his bones. The pain was so excruciating that he would plead with the doctors to kill him and put him out of his misery. But all that is behind him now. When I meet him, he looks calm and composed in a white kurta–pyjama, a blue turban and leather *jooties*. His left hand is still stiff but he can effortlessly drive a tractor through his paddy fields. When people like me ask him about the Battle of Phillora, those days of September 1965 flash before his eyes, and he is twenty-eight once again—the trigger-happy foul-mouthed gunner of Maj Singh. 'When I was running for help after the missile hit us, the Infantry guys who picked me up in their vehicle could not recognize me as my hair and skin had been charred. When I swore at them in Punjabi, they said, "*Aye tan 4 Horse da Vir Singh haiga* (This is Vir Singh of 4 Horse),"' he says, smiling widely.

Dfr Vir Singh speaks chaste Punjabi with a generous sprinkling of expletives but when he remembers Bhupinder sahab, his Squadron Commander, his voice softens. 'Memsahab used to cry when she visited him in Delhi Base Hospital where both of us were being treated,' he remembers. 'Bhupinder sahab would tell her to look at me. "*Dekh use, woh mujh se bhi buri tarah jala hai; himmat rakh* (Look at him, his burns are even worse than mine; be brave)," he would say.' Swr Vir Singh's condition was more critical than Maj Singh's. Even though the doctors would speak in English, he could follow what they were saying. '*Kehnde si, mar jayega, mar jayega* (They would whisper that he will not survive).' But Bhupinder sahab would scold them from his bed. '"*Aye mera gunner si. Tussi mar jana, mar jana kehnde. Bolo bacha lange* (He is my gunner. Don't say he might die. Say we'll save him)," he would say, telling me, "*Vir Singh, main tan zaroor ghar bhejanga* (Vir Singh, I will ensure you go back home)."' Maj Singh died the next Sunday, 3 October 1965. Swr Vir Singh survived and returned to his village after a year of treatment. '*Sab kismet da khel hai* (It is all destiny),' he says philosophically.

Brig Jasbir Singh (Retd) is seventy-four. As a strapping twenty-three-year-old way back in 1965, he was a Captain and the Officer in Charge of Reconnaissance Troops for 4 Horse (Hodson's Horse). While the squadrons moved in their Centurions, Capt Jasbir Singh would go around in his jeep, looking after regiment locations, food, troops and so on. 'It has been a long time,' he says, looking at the notes he has prepared for the interview, and points out places on the map to help me understand the Battle of Phillora better. With his friendly Labrador sprawled at his feet, he takes his time to patiently explain to me how the biggest tank battle that the Indian Army has fought unfolded that autumn.

3 September 1965

It is evening when the vehicles of 1 Armoured Division start moving down the road from Jalandhar to Pathankot.

Civilians gather by the roadside to wave to the men in black turbans, and slogans of '*Jai Jawan, Jai Kisan*' fill the air. There is excitement in the crowd; they are happy to see the Army moving to the border. Everyone wants Pakistan to be punished for its forays in Kashmir. Villagers generously offer food and water to the troops, some of whom have been travelling for days now. The advance party of 4 Horse has joined the convoy from Kapurthala. They are part of 1 Armoured Brigade and have received their orders to move in the afternoon. The advance party, led by Reconnaissance Troops leader Capt Jasbir Singh, has moved out at 4 p.m. The tanks and B vehicles (four-wheeled vehicles such as one-ton and three-ton trucks) are to follow by rail and road respectively.

'The entire division was moving, so there was a big jam on the roads that day. We reached Pathankot around 10 p.m.,' recounts Brig Jasbir Singh. 'Early next morning, we were told to move to the Kathua region and from there to Samba, where we were asked to make a harbour for the tanks.' The move has been so sudden that there are no maps available. Capt Jasbir Singh makes a quick sketch from the Brigade Major's map to know the area better. That night he is told that the 4 Horse tanks had been offloaded at Sarna and Madhopur around 40 km away and, in the absence of tank transporters, would be driven down. At 3 a.m. on 5 September, the stately Centurions start rolling in, fifteen at a time. The B-vehicle convoy of trucks arrives at first light. By then Commanding Officer (CO) Lt Col Madan Mohan Singh Bakshi, who had been on leave, also reaches the location. He is upset to see freshly planted paddy all around, increasing chances of the heavy tanks getting bogged down in the slushy fields. 'The Commandant was angry with me for having chosen that location as the tank harbour,' says Brig Jasbir. 'He cooled down only when I assured him that I had done my best despite not having any maps or familiarity with the area.'

For two days the men stay there. On the evening of 7 September, the entire 1 Armoured Brigade—with one Sherman regiment, 2 Lancers, and two Centurion regiments, 17 Horse and 16 Cavalry—receive orders to move into Pakistan. The battalion 4 Horse is made division reserve, which will be sent in to fight only if required. When gunner Vir Singh hears this, he swears loudly. '*Sahab, assi tan reserve vich reh gaye* (Sahab, we've been left behind),' he tells his tank Commander at which Maj Singh replies, '*Baari taan puttra twadi vi aa jaani hai, tey aani bhi aiddan hai ki yaad karoge tussi* (Son, your turn will come and you will remember it).' The advance starts on the morning of 8 September. At 6 a.m., the tanks of the two leading regiments—17 Horse and 16 Cavalry—cross the border. It is going well till 16 Cavalry reaches Chobara village. They come under heavy enemy fire and intense RT shelling; their first squadron of tanks is held up. The second squadron tries to outflank and bypass but their Squadron Commander Maj M.R. Sheikh's tank is shot down by the Pakistanis, killing him on the spot. This leads to complete confusion. The third squadron gets lost in the chaos and cannot be located. That is when 4 Horse is released as division reserve and told to replace 16 Cavalry. 'Around 10.30 a.m. we were asked to move up to village Chobara while 16 Cavalry was told to come back and reassemble,' recalls Brig

Jasbir. For the next two days 4 Horse stays in the area. On the evening of 10 September it starts raining heavily, which is bad news for the tanks. What makes it worse is that Pakistan does not have any metalled roads near the border, only mud tracks lined by thickets. That same night 4 Horse is ordered to sidestep to the Kotli Lalla area after dinner. Brig Jasbir remembers how they would get food only after dark. 'It was sent to us from behind; the langar party would camp wherever there was safety and water. Food would be cooked and packed there. It used to be supplied to us in the forward areas late at night. The men would keep it in their tanks and eat whenever hungry. Dinner was mostly dal, dry sabzi and puris, which we preferred to rotis because they didn't dry up and lasted longer. We would also get packed breakfast and lunch. When fresh food could not reach them, the men would make tea in their tanks and munch on dry rations like shakarparas which they used to carry.'

THE BATTLE OF PHILLORA

The plan to attack Phillora has been drawn up. The Armoured Brigade is to sidestep to the right in the area west of Kotli Lalla with 16 Cavalry on the right, 17 Horse in the centre and 4 Horse on the left (towards the east). The troops of 4 Horse have to cut off Phillora from the north-west and the west, from Wachoke and Saboke, and support the 43 Lorried Infantry Brigade attack from the north-west of Phillora Crossroads. At first light on 11 September, 1 Armoured Brigade has to advance and take Rurki Kalan, a task that is given to Charlie Squadron of 4 Horse. Thereafter, 4 Horse and 17 Horse are to encircle Phillora. The 16 Cavalry troops, who have lost many tanks, are told to protect the right flank and prevent enemy attacks, if any, from the Sialkot side.

On the morning of 11 September, C Squadron starts advancing towards Rurki Kalan village but it comes under severe enemy artillery and air attacks. Squadron Commander Maj C.B. Desraj Urs loses an eye to a shrapnel. However, he refuses to be evacuated and gallantly leads his tanks till they capture their objective, Rurki Kalan, which turns out to be a village of mud huts. Thereafter, he is evacuated and the command of his squadron falls on the young shoulders of 2Lt A.K. Nehra. Alpha and Bravo squadrons now move on either side of the village, making a dash for their objectives. A Squadron has to ensure that all enemy forces holding Chobara–Gadgor are intercepted and destroyed. Some sharp and intense tank-versus-tank encounters take place. The Centurions keep pushing forward resolutely, while the enemy tanks make a quick getaway to Phillora. The squadron has a field day, destroying eight Patton tanks and four jeeps fitted with recoilless guns. One of the jeeps that fall into their hands belongs to Capt Raza of Pakistan who is Officer Commanding, Recce Troops. Several maps are found in the jeep, which come in very handy.

CO's tank is hit

Moving between A and B squadrons is the Regimental Headquarters which includes the tanks of the Commanding Officer, the second in command and the Adjutant. Commanding Officer Lt Col Bakshi loses sight of the other tanks and, believing he has been left behind, starts moving at a faster pace to catch up. Around 10.30 a.m. he halts his tank and looks through his binoculars. He can clearly see the Phillora–Libbe road that is lined on both sides by tall sheesham trees. Suddenly, he spots six Patton tanks under the trees with their guns pointing towards Libbe. He realizes that he cannot escape unnoticed and decides to attack brazenly. He knocks down two of the tanks before they have time to react. Both go up in flames much to the delight of the Centurion crew. The enemy is quick to react and Lt Col Bakshi's tank comes under fire. He has by now engaged and destroyed two more tanks. But the enemy has also managed to hit his tank. He charges ahead at full speed and, crossing the road in a cloud of dust, passes between two blazing Pattons belching huge columns of smoke. His tank gets a direct hit this time and catches fire. He orders his crew to retrieve the Sten gun from the tank and bale out. The entire crew rushes into a sugar cane field, shooting with their pistols at the enemy. The Pakistanis chase them for a while and then give up.

While this scene is unfolding, Lt Col Bakshi's tank has naturally gone off the radar and therefore no one in 4 Horse has any inkling of what has transpired. However, B Squadron, under the command of Maj Singh, has advanced according to plan and is heading for Kotli Bagga and Dulmanwali, where it runs into enemy tanks. A fierce tank-versus-tank battle takes place and all hell breaks loose. There is a deafening noise of low-flying jets and loud explosions of bursting rockets within a few feet of their location. When pressure builds up on B Squadron, C Squadron joins them. They destroy a number of Pakistani tanks and the enemy's back is broken. Shortly after this harrowing experience, the welcome rumble of the 17 Horse tanks is heard from the direction of Libbe. Since the enemy has already fled, 17 Horse is able to advance unopposed through Libbe and on to Phillora. Lt Col Bakshi and his crew are picked up by the 17 Horse 2IC's tank and they return to the regiment after an absence of about four hours. Lt Col Bakshi assumes command from another tank after his brief adventure in the sugar cane fields.

Phillora falls

The armoured regiments 4 Horse and 17 Horse form a ring around Phillora, not only keeping the defences fully engaged, but also destroying tanks and Infantry trying to make a getaway. The stage is now set for 43 Lorried Infantry Brigade to attack Phillora. They do it with two battalions—5 Jat and 5/9 Gorkha Rifles. The 5 Jat cross the starting point at 6.45 a.m. and immediately come under a heavy air strike. When the enemy planes leave, intense enemy artillery fire starts. The airburst shells wreak havoc. They burst before hitting the ground and the casualties build up alarmingly. To make matters worse, the battalion loses most of its recoilless guns that get bogged down in the slushy ground. The Jats and Gorkhas, however, press on with the attack, supported by a squadron of 17 Horse.

5/9 Gorkha Rifles
April, 1965

Maj Gen Kartick Ganguly (Retd), author of a fascinating book called *Moments of Maximum Danger*, spends a quiet life in Kolkata now. He is seventy-five. Fifty years ago, when recall orders came for him in the wake of looming war clouds, he was in Calcutta to attend a family wedding. He took the first train to Jhansi where his battalion was located and reached there only to find that the troops had moved, leaving behind one officer to look after the families. That night the young Capt Ganguly boarded a special train that was packed with men and ammunition for the war. As he did not find a place to sit in any of the compartments, he got into the engine and took a seat on a steel plate attached to the side. He finally joined his battalion where they were camping near a village called Muchhal and took over Adjutant duties. For almost three months, nothing happened. The soldiers lived in their tents and settled down into a peacetime schedule, going about their tasks in a leisurely manner. In July, they were moved to a place called Hamira near Jalandhar, where the entire battalion camped inside a vacant brewery. In September, the 5/9 Gorkha Rifles Commanding Officer Lt Col Baldev Singh Grewal was called to the Brigade Commander's conference. He came back smiling. War orders had come. 'We had been told to enter Pakistan. The convoy would move at 8 p.m. the same night,' remembers Maj Gen Ganguly. Calling all the officers together, Lt Col Grewal gave them the good news. 'Gentlemen, we are going to war,' he said. Food was quickly prepared and packed for the next day; men started sending money home as they did not know when and if they would return. At 8 p.m. sharp, after a hearty dinner, the battalion was ready to move. They joined a long convoy of Army vehicles heading towards Samba on the Punjab–Jammu highway.

Reflections

Brig Jasbir Singh says there is always a shroud of fog around wars. What is planned on paper almost never happens on the ground. In Phillora, there were so many tank regiments on both sides that confusion was at its peak. He quotes an amusing incident that happened after the Indian Army had captured Phillora. 'I was in my jeep, watching things settle down after last light, when suddenly there was a din and a cry of "Tank, tank, tank." I saw four Pakistani tanks driving across Phillora. There were so many tanks around that no one noticed the Pakistani tanks which were trying to make a getaway. Before anyone could react, they had slunk past and moved to safety,' he laughs. Since he was in a jeep, he says he could have done nothing to stop them.

It's war

The Gorkhas drive through the night to reach Samba in the morning. There, they turn left and gather in the forest, awaiting further orders. The day passes uneventfully. Then, on the night of 6–7 September, they get orders to cross

the border around midnight. The plan is that in case the B
vehicles—one- and three-ton trucks—are not able to cross
the sugar cane fields, the Gorkhas will sit on the tanks of 16
Cavalry and go into Pakistan. The border outpost of Charwa
is captured during the night and the Infantry convoys move
ahead. Around 8 a.m. the next morning, Pakistani Sabre
jets start strafing the area. 'They would hit us every five
minutes. We would push our vehicles under the trees and
try to take cover. After the planes left, we would move on,'
says Maj Gen Ganguly. The other danger they face is from
the Mujahideens and Pakistani troops hiding in the sugar
cane fields, which let the tanks pass but open sniper fire
on the Infantry columns. 'It became such a nuisance that I
stopped my vehicle and told two of my jawans to fire our
light machine gun into the fields to chase them off. When we
went looking for them, they had disappeared leaving behind
heaps of fired cases,' he recounts. The Gorkhas camp under
the trees some distance from Charwa. Food supplies have
not reached them and the Commanding Officer tells them
that they can consume their emergency ration of chana and
gur.

On the afternoon of 8 September, the 5 Jat Adjutant, a
Vir Chakra from the 1962 war, visits the 5/9 Gorkha Rifles
Headquarters that has been set up under the trees. He wants
to know how Capt Ganguly is sending reports to the Brigade.
Capt Ganguly undoes his shirt buttons to show him the
notepad he is using. He tells him that he writes his reports in
English, which are converted to cipher by his signal operator
who in turn sends them to the radio operator who puts them
in Morse code and passes them on to the Brigade. The 5 Jat

Adjutant says he will do the same and prepares to go back to his battalion. As he walks towards his jeep, a sudden air attack targets the clump of trees where the two officers have been standing. Capt Ganguly tells the Jat officer to make a dash for the nearest trench. Even as he sprints towards it himself, right before his eyes a burst hits the 5 Jat Adjutant, slicing his head off. 'I will never forget the horror of watching him run a few steps, his body headless, after which he collapsed,' Maj Gen Ganguly says. After the planes pass, the men pick up the lifeless body of the young officer and place it in the same jeep that he had come in. The driver is weeping. 'What will I tell CO sahab?' he cries, but eventually leaves with the body.

Entering Libbe

On the night of 8–9 September, 5/9 Gorkha Rifles gets orders to move to a place called Libbe from where they and 5 Jat will attack Phillora Crossroads, which is the Divisional objective. Since the tanks have got bogged down in the ploughed fields, the move cannot happen the way it has been planned, but they have to keep on. To make matters worse, it starts raining at 8 p.m. and ankle-deep water soon collects in the fields. The vehicles grind to a halt. The Gorkhas get down, grit their teeth and start marching through the slush. They hang their 7.62 SLR rifles on their backs and carry their seven medium machine guns on their shoulders. Around 3 a.m. they reach close to Libbe. It has stopped raining by then. They know that once it is light, the air attacks will resume. They discover that the Jats, who were supposed to be on the left of the Sialkot–

Phillora–Jafarwal road, have not reached. Neither have the tanks. The batteries of their radio sets have died, so there is no way to find out what has happened. Since the attack had been scheduled for early morning, Lt Col Grewal orders his adjutant to go back to brigade headquarters and find out what the orders are for them now. Capt Ganguly runs all the way back. He finds the two Brigade Commanders—Brig K.K. Singh of 1 Armoured Brigade and Brig H.S. Dhillon of 43 Lorried Infantry Brigade—under a cluster of trees. They have hung a map of the area on the side of a vehicle and are discussing attack plans. Capt Ganguly learns that the Jats have got stuck somewhere and will take time to reach Libbe. The orders for 5/9 Gorkha Rifles are to reach their Forming Up Place (FUP) and await further orders, which the Brigade Commander will come and give personally. Ganguly goes back to his battalion. Around 11 a.m. on 9 September, the Gorkhas enter the village of Libbe. They see enemy tanks lined up on the road. Lt Col Grewal tells the Gorkhas to cross the road and make a dash for the sugar cane fields behind the tanks, company by company. They scamper across each time he blows his whistle, collect on the other side and await further orders, putting up a small flag to identify themselves. The enemy tanks fire at them and then start getting nervous since the Infantry seems to be building up behind them. They start moving out and the Indian armoured force encircling Phillora shoots some of them.

Around 11.30 a.m., Brig H.S. Dhillon, Brigade Commander of 43 Lorried Infantry Brigade, and Brigade Major Maj Ravi Mahajan locate 5/9 Gorkha Rifles. The

Brigade Commander tells them that 5 Jat and the bogged down tanks will take time to reach but the attack cannot be postponed. He orders 5/9 Gorkha Rifles to attack Phillora Crossroads with all the companies spread out. The battalion walks down to its FUP, about 730 metres short of Phillora. It is around 2 p.m. Hungry stomachs start to growl but the Gorkhas have eaten nothing but sugar cane for six days. Not only are they hungry, they have also gone without water for a long time. The moment they spot a well with a bucket and rope by its side, they rush to it and start filling up their bottles. Just then enemy shelling begins. In the excitement of having found water, the soldiers have not noticed the Pakistanis sitting atop masjids in the village, directing fire at them. Bullets start hitting the men and there are some casualties. Commanding Officer Lt Col Grewal is livid. He picks up a cane and starts hitting his men, forcing them to get back immediately. He then orders *chaggal*s to be filled up by each company by stealth and the men quench their thirst.

At 3 p.m. the Gorkhas attack Phillora Crossroads. While C and D companies attack from the right of the Sialkot–Jafarwal road, B Company attacks from the left. A Company, which Capt Ganguly is commanding, goes along the road, accompanied by the Commanding Officer. A tough fight follows. The Gorkhas are making good progress, when a lone enemy tank that starts firing at the advancing troops halts the assault. It is spewing fire and not letting the men move ahead. An exasperated Lt Col Grewal orders Capt Ganguly to do something about this unexpected hindrance. Capt Ganguly assumes that the attacking tank cannot see the area immediately behind it, so he ducks into the sugar cane fields and slowly makes his way to its rear. Moving steadily and quietly, he climbs on top and, opening its cupola, flings two grenades inside, one after the other. After a while, he gingerly opens the hatch. A thick plume of smoke gushes out. Once that clears, Capt Ganguly lowers himself in and finds a lone Pakistani soldier lying dead inside. He is a Dafadar. He salutes the dead man for his courage in single-handedly stalling an Infantry attack and then, pushing him aside, gets into the driver's seat. 'I thought I would drive the tank to my own side and we could use it, but it did not start,' he says. He then realizes why it has been standing there. It has broken down and has obviously not been able to accompany its squadron that has probably pushed on to Chawinda where the Pakistanis are now collecting for a final defence. When Capt Ganguly climbs out of the tank, he finds that an Indian tank has driven up and a Sikh officer with a black turban and headgear is pointing a pistol at him. The Centurion has come to investigate the Patton and has mistaken him for an enemy soldier. When Capt Ganguly identifies himself, the Sikh officer lowers his weapon and drives away. A jubilant Capt Ganguly returns to his men and gets a warm welcome from his Commanding Officer and the Brigade Major, who has stayed with them through the attack, helping them communicate with the Brigade and the Division through the wireless set in his jeep.

Phillora Crossroads is captured by 4.30 p.m. but an immediate tank counter-attack from the Pakistanis comes at 5 p.m. from the Chawinda side. This is also beaten back by the Gorkhas. The Brigade Major asks for tank support. 'We could hear the tanks coming and an exchange of fire took place but we did not budge from our position,' says Maj Gen Ganguly. Half an hour later, the enemy tanks and Infantry withdraw. By 5.30 pm the Jats also arrive and are deployed east of the Crossroads. They also take up defensive positions and the two battalions prepare to defend Phillora from enemy counter-attacks that night. Counter-attacks are expected before dawn and they know that if they can hold on to the occupied position through the night, history will be made. They then start looking for injured soldiers who are brought in on a recovery tank and an ambulance sent by the Jats. Bleeding from gunshot or shelling wounds, these soldiers are carried into a big hall in the rest house at Phillora. Since doctors, medicines and bandages have not reached yet, Ganguly orders that sweet milky tea be made in a biscuit tin and served to them every half hour.

Till the next morning Pakistan keeps sending jitter parties but eventually they all withdraw. The battle is over. The enemy collapse at Phillora is so sudden that the higher commanders of the enemy side do not even seem to be aware of it. Within half an hour of Indian troops occupying Phillora, an enemy helicopter arrives and is shot down by Maj Birender Singh of 17 Horse as it tries to land. An intercepted message indicates that their 'Bada Imam' has been killed. He is understood to be the General Officer Commanding, belonging either to 15 Infantry Division or 6 Armoured Division. By the end of the battle, 5/9 Gorkha Rifles has thirty-four killed and 174 wounded in action. Maj Gen Rajinder Singh Sparrow, MVC, General Officer Commanding, 1st Armoured Division, makes a visit to Phillora amidst continuous enemy shelling to personally congratulate the troops of all units on their victory.

A decisive victory

On 12 September 1965, the tank battle at Phillora ended in an important, decisive victory for the Indian Army, with the Pakistani forces retreating. Lt Gen Harbaksh Singh, VrC, has said in his book *War Despatches* that the Battle of Phillora would always rank high in the annals of armoured warfare—a glowing tribute to the skilful junior leadership and astonishingly accurate gunnery the soldiers displayed.

According to ex-Pakistan Army Major (retd) and military historian A.H. Amin, 'Phillora was captured by the Indians at 1530 hours on 11th September. 11 Cavalry (Pakistan) fought well but lost so many tanks that from 11th September onwards it ceased to function as a complete tank regiment.' In the Battle of Phillora, 4 Horse won forty-three gallantry awards, including two Maha Vir Chakras for Maj Bhupinder Singh (posthumously) and Lt Col M.M.S. Bakshi. They also got the Battle Honour Phillora and the Theatre Honour Punjab. Lt Col A.B. Tarapore, Commandant, 17 Horse, was posthumously decorated with the Param Vir Chakra, India's highest gallantry award. The 5/9 Gorkha Rifles was given the Battle Honour Phillora.

The continued thrust by the Indian Army into Pakistani territory culminated in the Battle of Chawinda. On 22 September the United Nations Security Council unanimously passed a resolution that called for an unconditional ceasefire by both countries. When the war ended the following day, India had occupied almost 518 sq km of Pakistani territory in the Sialkot sector, including the villages of Phillora, Pagowal, Maharajke, Gadgor and Bajagrahi—all of which were returned to Pakistan after the Tashkent Declaration.

Ball of fire

On 19 September, Maj Bhupinder Singh's Bravo Squadron is ordered to advance across the Sialkot–Chawinda railway line and towards Sodreke to protect the right flank of the regiment. After crossing the railway line, they run into enemy tanks and come under heavy artillery fire. Maj Singh's tank is hit by a Patton and catches fire. 'There were four men inside, but we managed to extricate all of them unharmed,' remembers his gunner Dfr Vir Singh. Having brought the fire under control, the Major goes into action again. His tank manages to knock down four enemy tanks. At about 5 p.m., his tank is hit by a ball of fire. Vir Singh says he had never seen anything like it before. It rips apart the tank's gun and burns alive the driver who doesn't even get a chance to get up from his seat. Maj Singh manages to pull out his loader from the turret, which has become an inferno, but is badly burned himself. The heat has singed Vir Singh's hair and skin and charred the clothes off his body. He is left sightless and in his briefs, with a molten *kada* clinging to his wrist. Both are evacuated and treated first at Pathankot and later at Army Base Hospital, Delhi. While Vir Singh recovers, Maj Singh succumbs to his injuries. Later, 4 Horse realizes that the ball of fire was a Cobra missile that was powerful enough to cut through armour with its extreme heat. Maj Singh is posthumously awarded the Maha Vir Chakra, independent India's second highest gallantry award.

. . .

During the capture of Phillora, a splinter cuts through
LT COL ARDESHIR BURZORJI TARAPORE's arm
leaving a gaping wound. He refuses to be evacuated,
insisting it is 'just a scratch'. Besides, he still has to oversee
the attack on Chawinda. In this battle, his tank is hit
several times. Inspired by his leadership, the regiment
fiercely attacks and destroys as many as sixty enemy tanks.

Lt Col Ardeshir Burzorji Tarapore
Param Vir Chakra

September 1965

The tanks of 17 Horse (Poona Horse) have crossed the border; they have fought the Battle of Phillora and are now deployed in Sialkot district of Pakistan's Punjab province. Commanding Officer Lt Col Ardeshir Burzorji Tarapore, fondly called Adi in his regiment, calls his 2IC Maj Niranjan Singh Cheema (later Lt Gen Cheema [Retd]) aside. Maj Cheema, who is expecting a war briefing, is taken aback by what his Commanding Officer tells him. 'If I die in the war, I must be cremated on the battlefield,' Lt Col Tarapore tells him. 'My prayer book must be given to my mother, my gold chain to my wife, my ring to my daughter, my bracelet and pen to my son. And Niranjan, please tell my son Xerxes to join the Army.' Five days later, Lt Col Tarapore is fatally wounded after being hit by an enemy artillery shell.

Many years later, giving an interview to a leading English daily, Gen Cheema wondered if Lt Col Tarapore, who was a deeply religious man, had had a premonition about his death. On 16 September 1965, during the fierce tank battle fought between India and Pakistan in the Sialkot sector, an enemy shell hit Lt Col Tarapore's tank. He was standing in the cupola when the tank erupted in flames consuming him and his intelligence officer. He died a hero's death right there in the battlefield, much to the shock of the men he loved so fondly. At that time his left arm was in a sling from an earlier war injury for which he had stubbornly refused to be evacuated. He had led his men right into Pakistan and his unit had successfully captured Jassoran and Buttar Dograndi.

Zarine Mahir Boyce is in her sixties now and it has been fifty years since her father, Lt Col Ardeshir Burzorji Tarapore, died, but his memories are still fresh in her mind. Sitting in her Pune house, she remembers the loving dad and brave soldier that he was. Sometimes a smile surfaces in her voice and sometimes it is tinged with sadness. It has been many years, she says, but it still seems like it happened just the other day. The first time her father did not come back home, leaving the entire family worried, she was just fifteen, she remembers.

It was January 1964. The sun had set and in the beautiful house in Babina cantonment where the Tarapores lived, the lights came on. There was cake on the dining table to celebrate the birthday of a house guest, but Mrs Perin Tarapore was still waiting for her husband to come back. She was starting to get worried because he had promised to be back home early. The kids, Xerxes and Zarine, were getting impatient too, but there was no sign of their father.

At 7.45 p.m., Mrs Tarapore was relieved to hear a vehicle pulling up in their driveway. It was her husband's jeep. When it stopped outside their porch, she was shocked to see Lt Col Tarapore stepping out, his uniform caked in slush. His driver and wireless operator were similarly covered in grime. The kids and the guests had gathered around him by then and he apologetically explained to the group that his jeep had got stuck in the Gurari nullah just outside Babina. His uniform had got soiled because he had helped his men push it out of the slush. One of the house guests, already impressed with Lt Col Tarapore's rank, stared in disbelief. How could he, the Commanding Officer of his regiment, get into the water to push the jeep forward? The normally gentle and polite Colonel stiffened at that and retorted, 'I am not made of sugar and salt that I would get washed away. Anything my men do, I do with them.'

A born soldier

Adi was born on 18 August 1923 in Bombay. It is believed that the family name, Tarapore, came from the village of Tarapore which was one of 100 hamlets in the *mansab* awarded by Shivaji to an ancestor of Adi's who used to be a leader under the Maratha ruler eight generations ago. The mansab had been awarded as a token of appreciation for his courage and loyalty and, incidentally, these were the very qualities Adi displayed right from childhood.

An anecdote related to me dates back to Lt Col Tarapore's childhood. He was all of six, and was playing with his ten-year-old sister, Yadgar, in their backyard. The family cow broke loose and charged at Yadgar. While Yadgar screamed in terror, little Adi quickly picked up a stick and, stepping in front of the cow, smacked it on the nose with it. The startled animal turned tail and fled, and the two children returned to their game. This quality of fearlessness was only burnished with time. In those days Hyderabad was a separate state and though after leaving school Adi had his heart set upon joining the armoured regiment, he was commissioned into 7 Hyderabad Infantry as a Second Lieutenant in January 1942.

Tarapore got Poona Horse quite by chance. Once when his battalion was being inspected by Maj Gen El-Edros, the Commander-in-Chief of the Indian State Forces, during the routine grenade-throwing training a young sepoy panicked and accidentally lobbed his grenade right into the throwing bay. Without a thought for his own safety, Tarapore immediately jumped in, picked up the grenade and flung it away. The grenade burst as it left his hand, and flying shrapnel got embedded in his chest but there were no casualties. Maj Gen El-Edros was very impressed with the young officer and once Tarapore recovered from his injuries, called him to his office to congratulate him. Tarapore requested him for a transfer to an armoured regiment, and Maj Gen El-Edros had him posted to 1 Hyderabad Imperial Service Lancers.

Tarapore was posted to the armoured regiment 17 Horse (Poona Horse) after the merger of Hyderabad State with the Union of India. There he joined A Squadron, which was primarily a Rajput squadron, and despite being a non-Rajput, developed such a close rapport with the men that he was jokingly given the unofficial designation of 'Colonel of A Squadron'. In fact, he even started growing the fearsome cavalier moustache, modelling it on senior Squadron Non-Commissioned Officer Bahadur Singh's handlebar. When he commanded the regiment many years later, he continued to sport this impressive moustache. He was fond of saying that the Commandant of Poona Horse only looked like a Commandant if he sported a cavalier moustache.

The two qualities of Lt Col Tarapore that all his men and officers testify to are that he was fearless and a hands-on Commanding Officer. No task was too menial for him. He often surprised soldiers by personally helping them load ammunition on to tanks, something that most other officers did not do. Seventy-one-year-old Swr Nathu Singh (Retd), remembers the time when Centurion tanks had recently been introduced to the regiment. Nathu was driving a Centurion, when the engine started making a loud, rattling noise, confusing him completely. Lt Col Tarapore, who had been watching from afar, quickly sprinted up to him and jumped on to the cupola of the tank. He then gently told Nathu, *'Baccha, raise kam karo.'* He was the officer who had gone abroad, received training and acquired Centurion tanks for the unit and no one knew them better than he did.

The time of reckoning

The regiment 17 Horse was at Kapurthala when war was declared and they were told to move to a village ahead of Samba. That was where they received orders to cross the border through the Pakistani village of Barkania. It had rained during the night and the fields were slushy. The children were going to school and women were on their way to fill water, when they were surprised to see battle tanks splashing past them through the mud. They stood and watched in awe, waving to the men in black dungarees who were standing upright in open cupolas, mistaking them for Pakistanis. Some called out to the soldiers who smiled back at them, while others just gaped at the forty-five monster machines rumbling past languidly, one behind the other.

What the Pakistani villagers did not know was that these were the feared Centurions of Poona Horse. Lt Col Tarapore had given strict instructions that civilians were not to be harmed. 'Our fight is with the Army. We shall not touch any innocent men, women or children,' was what he had said, his voice crackling through the wireless sets. All the men could hear it. And that was why the villagers had mistaken them for friendly Pakistani soldiers.

The Battle of Phillora

The Battle of Phillora started on 10 September with the Indian troops advancing to launch a massive attack. On 11 September 1965, Poona Horse was assigned the task of delivering the main armoured thrust for capturing Phillora.

It decided upon launching a surprise attack on Phillora from the rear. The 1st Armoured Division, equipped with four armoured regiments, of which Poona Horse was one, was on the offensive in the area. With no resistance from the enemy, the tanks kept rolling into Pakistan. 'At 11 a.m. the first air attack came. Till then the enemy had no idea that we had gone so far into their country,' chuckles Gen Ajai Singh (Retd), who was a young Captain of the C Squadron of Poona Horse at the time. Pakistan surprised the advancing Army by sudden strafing and the air attacks did more damage to lorry and Infantry columns than to the tanks. Gen Ajai Singh remembers, however, that the toll was heavy for the other armoured battalions. There was complete chaos. Many of the men who were standing in their cupolas were hit and just collapsed or were grievously injured.

The Patton tanks of Pakistan were facing the armoured units 16 Cavalry and 4 Horse (Hodson's Horse). It was at this time that on Lt Col Tarapore's initiative, Poona Horse moved in to stabilize the situation. As was typical of him, he did not wait for instructions and attacked the Pakistanis without warning. 'And what a ferocious attack it was!' says the old General looking back on that smoke-filled morning with pride. 'We destroyed thirteen tanks at the first go.' For two days, intense fighting continued and the Pakistani soldiers were forced to beat a retreat towards Chawinda. The Indians captured Phillora on 11 September. Pakistan's 11 Cavalry fought well but lost so many tanks that it ceased to function as a complete tank regiment. Lt Col Tarapore was wounded in the operation. A splinter cut through his arm leaving a gaping wound. His immobile arm was put in a sling.

After the capture of Phillora, the Brigade Commander and General Officer Commanding came over to congratulate Poona Horse. Immediate awards were discussed but Lt Col Tarapore brushed them off, saying his regiment was just doing its duty. He refused to be evacuated, insisting that the wound was 'just a scratch'. Besides, he still had to oversee the attack on Chawinda.

The Pak forces regrouped for a last fight at Chawinda.

The capture of Buttar Dograndi

The plan was that the Infantry would attack Chawinda on the afternoon of 16 September and Poona Horse would encircle it. The task was given to C Squadron. Gen Ajai Singh remembers how his squadron's tanks started moving in with 9 Garhwal in support. The Indian Army did not realize that six Pakistani tanks were already hiding under cover in Buttar Dograndi, which was on the way, and that they were prepared for the attack. When C Squadron's tanks broke cover to attack the village, the Pakistani Pattons shot six out of ten on the spot. Since the enemy was hidden and the Poona Horse tanks had to move out of the sugar cane fields and expose themselves for the attack, the situation quickly took a turn for the worse for the Indian side. Capt Ajai Singh called Lt Col Tarapore on the wireless. 'I asked him for immediate reinforcements, because otherwise we would have lost Buttar Dograndi.' Lt Col Tarapore immediately moved in with his own tank while directing A Squadron to join the battle as well. While the Pakistani Pattons were well hidden amidst the trees in the village 1 km away, the Indian tanks had broken cover for the attack. It was a daring plan but together the nine Centurions—which included five of Capt Ajai Singh, three of A Squadron and one of Commanding Officer Tarapore—attacked the Pattons and destroyed all six of them. Buttar Dograndi had been captured. It was a moment of celebration for Poona Horse and its Commanding Officer. In this battle, his own tank was hit several times. Inspired by his leadership, the regiment fiercely attacked and destroyed as many as sixty enemy tanks, suffering only nine tank casualties.

A freak shell

Lt Col Tarapore is relaxed that evening. The daring capture of Buttar Dograndi is fresh in his mind and he is feeling quite proud of the men he commands. The battle is still raging, but he knows it is just a matter of time before Pakistan caves in. Standing at his tank hatch, he is watching the battlefield, a cup of tea in his right hand, his left arm still in a sling. He is discussing the situation with his intelligence officer who is to his right. It is typical of him to stand in the open, unguarded, giving instructions or just surveying the area. At that unfortunate moment, a freak shell comes and hits his tank, setting it on fire instantly. Both Tarapore and his intelligence officer are engulfed in the flames. They have taken a direct hit.

Capt Ajai Singh is evacuating a gunner who has fallen off his tank, and he freezes when he hears from his operator that the Commanding Officer has been hit. When he manages to reach the spot, he finds his Commanding

Officer's lifeless body laid out on the ground, bathed in the orange rays of the setting sun; his soldiers stand around him, mourning. While the late Lt Col Tarapore's body is tearfully taken back home, his disabled tank, Khushab, named after a famous battle honour where Poona Horse was awarded two Victoria Crosses, has to be left behind. For the boldness and valour displayed by him in six continuous days of fierce tank battle, Lt Col Ardeshir Burzorji Tarapore is awarded the Indian Army's highest wartime gallantry award, the Param Vir Chakra, posthumously.

The Battle of Barki

Courtesy: History Division, Ministry of Defence

On the western border of Punjab lies the town of Ferozepur. To get here you head west from Ludhiana and keep driving along National Highway 71—a beautiful tarred road, on both sides of which bright pink bougainvillea blooms and endless green fields of wheat rustle in the wind. Drive down late in the afternoon and you have the orange glow of the setting sun in your eyes all the way. Because you're heading west—towards Pakistan. In Ferozepur cantonment stands a modest red sandstone structure on which you find inscribed the words 'Barki 10 September 1965'. Next to it are a Pakistani Patton tank and a milestone that says Lahore 15.

The Barki memorial was constructed in 1969 to salute the soldiers of 7 Infantry Division who made the supreme sacrifice on the battlefield on 10 September 1965 and paved the way for the fall of Barki, a Pakistani town about 24 km south-east of Lahore. It is also a reminder of just how close to Lahore the Indian forces had advanced in the Pak-provoked war of 1965.

Most people have never heard of Ferozepur. It is one of those places that fell off the map in 1947 and has been lying forgotten since, buried under a pile of history and the memories of old sardars who squat by the roadside at dusk, sipping steaming cups of milky tea. Yet, fifty years ago, Ferozepur was where the units 16 Punjab, 4 Sikh and 9 Madras were when they received orders to load their trucks and reach Khalra, the last village on the Pakistan border. They were asked to cross the border, take over the village of Barki, go right up to Ichhogil Canal and threaten Lahore. The aim was to scare Pakistan into abandoning its plans to occupy Kashmir. I heard the amazing story of the battle from two officers who fought in Barki—Col Manmohan Singh (Retd) from 16 Punjab, who in 1965 was Lt Manmohan Singh, Bravo Company Commander, and Brig Kanwaljit Singh (Retd) from 4 Sikh who was Lt Kanwaljit Singh, Delta Company Commander, at the time. Both officers, now past seventy, were in their early twenties when they fought the war. I traced Col Manmohan Singh at his small flat in a village near Solan where he spends his summers, while Brig Kanwaljit Singh directed my taxi right up to his quietly elegant Gurgaon house: 'On your right there will be a park and on your left a white house, outside which you will find a handsome *banda*,' he said. Almost there, I looked left and found a dashing Sikh officer with a salt-and-pepper beard standing there, smiling broadly. It was the man who had led his company to victory in Barki and written two books about it. Here is the story of that great battle as recounted by these two brave and spirited soldiers.

5 September 1965

It is a sultry September in Ferozepur though the mornings are cool. At 5 a.m. sharp, the soldiers get into their trucks and an unending convoy of olive green winds its way down the road that will take them to Khalra. As they cross the wheat fields, the sound of the azan from a nearby mosque, carried by the wind, reaches their ears. Some of the soldiers look ahead quietly, remembering families they are leaving behind; others wave to the farmers toiling in the fields. At the bridge in Harike close to where the rivers Beas and Sutlej meet, they watch the waterbirds drying their wings in the sun. From there the convoy takes the old road to Lahore. By the time night falls, they are at Khalra. 'Since 3 September we had been on four-hour notice to move for an undisclosed task at an undisclosed location. War clouds had been looming and letters had been sent to soldiers and officers on leave to join back. However, our men had been hearing the news on the radio and had started coming back on their own,' remembers a nostalgic Brig Kanwaljit Singh.

The 7 Infantry Division, which includes 48 Infantry Brigade and 65 Infantry Brigade, as well as Central India Horse, an armoured unit with Sherman tanks, has chalked out the attack plan. The strategy is that on the morning of 6 September, the battalions 4 Sikh (65 Infantry Brigade) and 6/8 Gorkha Rifles (48 Infantry Brigade) will cross the border and occupy Pakistan's border outposts and hold a safe firm base; then 48 Infantry Brigade will clear the area up to Barki.

After a night's rest, on 6 September, as is the plan, 4 Sikh swings into action. Alpha Company, led by Maj Shamsher Singh Manhas, and Bravo Company, led by Maj Dilip Singh

Sidhu, capture two border outposts on the right side of the road. On the left of the road, 6/8 Gorkha Rifles also captures a border outpost. A secure foothold to attack Pakistan is established. Halfway between Khalra and Barki runs an old drain called Hudiara where a village of the same name is situated. Hudiara is well defended by Pakistan. The 48 Infantry Brigade, which has been tasked with capturing Barki that evening, reaches Hudiara but cannot cross the drain because of intensive shelling by the enemy. A plan is made to eliminate the opposition under cover of darkness. However, Pakistan pre-empts it and, just before the attack can happen, they blow up the bridge, vacate the defences and disappear into the night. The Indian soldiers watch the bridge burning, the orange flames licking the purple sky. 'They did well,' Col Manmohan Singh acknowledges grudgingly to me. 'They made sure that our tanks could not cross over.' The next day, the Infantry crosses the Hudiara drain. 'We waded through the water which was barely a foot and a half deep, but since the drain was about 50 ft wide, our tanks couldn't cross it,' he says. The engineers are called and they get on with the task of constructing a new bridge for the tanks. Assisted by two companies of 4 Sikh, they keep working despite continued shelling by Pakistan. Right before Lt Kanwaljit Singh's eyes, a bomb hits L/Nk Mangal Singh who is blown to bits, splattering Lt Singh with his blood and flesh. For the young soldiers, the violence of war is still sinking in. By evening the bridge is complete but when it is inspected, it is found that the span is not sufficient for the tanks to cross over. It is a disheartening situation but Lt Col S.C. Joshi, Commanding Officer, Central India

Horse, goes to the demolished bridge, asks his men to fill in the gaps, and boldly takes his own tank first across the drain. The rest follow and, by the time the sun rises on 8 September, the tanks of Central India Horse are on the other side of the Hudiara drain.

Bodies and blood

Brig Kanwaljit Singh remembers the morning after the capture of Barki. It was 8.30 a.m. and he was in a trench with Lt B.S. Chahal who had been officiating as Adjutant and had killed a Pakistani Junior Commissioned Officer manning a pillbox, when he realized his throat was parched. 'I asked for water and the jawans got me some in a tumbler. When I had a sip, it tasted strange. That's when I saw that the water was reddish in colour. I asked the men where they had got it from, and they showed me a pond close to our trench. There were bodies of enemy soldiers and dead animals lying all around it; some had even fallen into the water. Their blood had turned the water red. I was so thirsty that I just closed my eyes and took two sips from the tumbler before returning it,' he says.

Securing the flanks

Early on 8 September, 4 Sikh is ordered to clear the village of Brahmanabad on the left side of the road. Delta Company, led by Lt Kanwaljit Singh, makes a bold frontal

attack supported by artillery fire. Alpha Company, under
the command of Maj Shamsher Singh Manhas, is tasked
with clearing the area up to the village of Barka Kalan. As
the assaulting companies close in, the Pakistanis bring in
heavy artillery airbursts but soon desert the villages and
retreat. However, due to intense enemy artillery fire, one
Junior Commissioned Officer of Delta Company and
three jawans from 4 Sikh are killed in the daring daylight
attack, while many are injured. The troops of 16 Punjab
also face heavy shelling. 'In military parlance we call it
carpet bombing—they bombed every inch of the terrain.
Luckily, we had dug our trenches during the night, so
we just got into those and lay low with our heads down
and our morale up, hearing the bombs explode around
us,' remembers Col Singh. The units are now tasked
with securing the right and left flanks of Barki. These
are the villages of Barka Kalan or Barki Major (to the left
of the road to Barki) and Barka Khurd or Barki Minor
(to the right of the same road). Commanded by Lt Col
B.K. Satyan, 9 Madras launches a daylight attack on
Barka Kalan. It is a ferocious fight in which they lose six
men but capture the village. Then, 16 Punjab launches
a night attack on Barka Khurd. 'We did it without
much opposition,' remembers Col Singh. 'Pakistan had
concentrated on defending Barka Kalan and there were
just a few snipers in Barka Khurd who fired at us and
then retreated. We could take over the village without any
casualties.' The Pakistani troops have retreated to Barki
and are bombing the area. A big, bloody battle is waiting
to happen.

The attack plan

The 9th of September is particularly hot. But even in the scorching heat the Sikhs remain in the slit trenches they have dug because the enemy is acutely sensitive to movement and starts shelling the area at the slightest stirring. To augment their artillery fire, the Pakistanis innovate by lowering the sights of their anti-aircraft guns and using these for ground-level fire. The guns prove deadly, their shells bursting with deadly accuracy. 'The sun was burning overhead and the trenches were suffocating. We were also very thirsty but the troops showed excellent water discipline. No one stirred because of the shelling. Luckily, there were sugar cane fields around us and later we discovered a small pond from which we could draw drinking water,' says Brig Kanwaljit Singh. Food comes late at night; some manage to eat, some don't. The intense firing makes movement difficult. The night finds 16 Punjab well entrenched in Barka Khurd, 9 Madras in Barka Kalan and 4 Sikh simmering in their slit trenches along the right of the road. Patrols are sent to obtain information about the enemy defences but have to return since the Pakistanis have lit up no man's land and are firing shells and illuminating tracers at any kind of movement.

On the morning of 10 September, Lt Col Anant Singh, Commanding Officer, 4 Sikh, is called to the Brigade headquarters which has been established near Hudiara. Brigade Commander Brig Lerb Ferris takes him to the Division HQ. There they are met by General Officer Commanding, 7 Infantry Division, Maj Gen H.K. Sibal and Corps Commander

Lt Gen J.S. Dhillon. 'Col Anant Singh later told me that Gen Dhillon was very annoyed with the tardy movement of the division. The General felt our movement was very slow. We must get Barki, come what may, he said,' recounts Brig Kanwaljit Singh. Lt Col Anant Singh is a battle-hardy soldier. He takes on the challenge and volunteers to attack, telling the Corps Commander, '4 Sikh will give you Barki.'

Battle plans are quickly drawn up. Barki shall be attacked in two phases. The troops of 4 Sikh will attack and capture the village in the night in the first phase. The Sherman tanks of Central India Horse will lead the attack in an unorthodox manner with all lights on, all weapons firing on target; 4 Sikh will follow and capture Barki physically. Once they have met their objective, phase two will be launched. Two companies of 16 Punjab will move in through Barki and secure both banks of Ichhogil Canal. After the banks are captured, a third company will cross the bridge on the canal and establish a bridgehead on the other side to stop counter-attacks by the enemy. The company shall then blow up the bridge and swim across the 140-ft-wide canal to Barki, bringing back the injured if they can.

ATTACK ON BARKI

It is the afternoon of 10 September. A slight wind has started blowing. Since the enemy fire has eased up a bit, the Sikhs quickly come out of their trenches and fill up their bottles with water from the pond. The O group, which includes the Company Commanders and specialist Platoon Commanders, then gathers around the Commanding Officer, who has returned from the Division headquarters late that afternoon. They are eager to know what has been decided. Lt Col Anant Singh speaks to them, his voice strong and full of confidence. In chaste Punjabi, he outlines the daring attack that is going to take place that night. He tells them they are fortunate to have got a chance to return to the homes they were forced to leave at the time of the Partition. *'Saddi kismet bahut changi aa. Aaj mauka mileya wapas apne gharaun nu jan da. Aaj hathiyan naal saddi barat jaugi aur aisi aatishbazi hoyegi ke diwali vi picche pai jaugi. Barki dulhan di tarah hai. Tussi aaj dulhe ho. Sheron, tagde ho jao. Aaj Barki vihaoni hai* (We are very fortunate that today we have got a chance to go back to our homes. Tanks shall lead our wedding procession like elephants. There will be so much firing that Diwali shall pale in comparison. Today, you are the bridegrooms. Barki is your bride. My lions, be strong. Today we have to capture Barki).'

The men are raring to go. It is decided that Alpha Company, under Maj Shamsher Singh Manhas, and Charlie Company, under officiating Company Commander Sub Sadhu Singh, will attack Barki. C Company will be accompanied by medium machine-gun Platoon Commander Lt Hari Singh with machine guns. Bravo Company, under Maj D.S. Sidhu, will be in reserve. Delta Company, under Lt Kanwaljit Singh, is given a special task. He and his men will wait at Mile 16, about 1.8 km from Barki. He will rendezvous with the tanks of Central India Horse at 7.30 p.m. The tanks will be followed by civilian trucks laden with wooden planks. Delta Company will get into the trucks and move forward with them. There is a drain that they must cross just before Barki. Delta Company's task is to ignore the enemy fire that is expected to come at them, and quickly fill up the drain with the wooden planks so that the tanks can cross over.

'My Commanding Officer had told me to expect 100 per cent casualties but the task had to be done. There will be intense firing from the enemy but you will keep chucking planks into the drain till it fills up, and thereafter capture the area left of the road, he had said,' remembers Brig Kanwaljit Singh.

Mile 16, 7.20 p.m.

Night has fallen when Lt Kanwaljit Singh and Delta Company (about 100-plus in strength) reach Mile 16. They reach ten minutes before the given time, rifles slung across their chests, the reassuring weight of ammunition packs pressing against their backs, grenades hanging from their belts. They wait impatiently for the tanks to arrive but the night remains dark and silent. Time ticks slowly by. At 7.50 p.m., they watch the attacking companies—Alpha and Charlie—forming up on the right of the road. It appears as if the enemy has come to know of their plan as the entire area is targeted with artillery fire. As the shells start exploding dangerously close to his men, Lt Col Anant Singh orders them to move 180-odd metres closer to Barki to escape the shelling. Minutes seem like hours and the soldiers start getting restless. They listen anxiously for the rumble and clatter of the tanks but till 8 p.m. there is no sign of the Shermans. Finally, Lt Col Singh decides they will not wait any longer. The attack must be launched. He is confident that the tanks will show up eventually. He asks the artillery to start shelling Barki and the men break into a brisk walk, adrenaline coursing through their veins. Known as the Saragarhi battalion, 4 Sikh is famous for the valour with which twenty-one of their men had fought off more than 10,000 Afghan and Orakzai tribesmen on 12 September 1897. Every single man had fought till death in this suicidal defence of the village of Saragarhi, which is now in Pakistan, and had been awarded the Indian Order of Merit, the highest gallantry award of the time, equivalent to the Param Vir Chakra. It is September again. The time has come to display that valour one more time.

While Lt Kanwaljit Singh and his men continue to wait for the tanks near Mile 16, Alpha and Charlie companies run into the pillboxes Pakistan has designed for Barki's defence. It had been expected that Barki would be well defended but just how well defended it is, the Sikhs find out that dark night. Pakistan has two companies (plus elements of their Recce and Support Battalion) in Barki village and the Ichhogil Canal area. They also have eleven pillboxes scattered all around. The pillboxes are a new concept in bunkers. Made of concrete and steel, they are like rooms with thick walls and roofs. The walls have loopholes through which guns can be fired. Each pillbox is manned by at least three soldiers operating a medium machine gun, a light machine gun and a Sten gun. The bunker is stocked with plenty of ammunition and grenades. 'Even our 25-pounder guns could not have any effect on these pillboxes, while anti-tank guns could only make a dent on the structure,' says Col Manmohan Singh. The only way to neutralize them is to physically enter the pillboxes with complete disregard for one's own life and that is what the braves of 4 Sikh do. Hand-to-hand fights break out in the Mud Hut area, 274 metres from Barki. The men crawl up to the pillboxes, disable them manually by throwing grenades into the bunkers; there are abuses interspersed with cries of pain from those who have been hit. The enemy fights desperately but the valiant Sikhs don't give way. Pakistan targets the men with staggering artillery fire. As many as 2500 shells are fired within forty-five minutes, but the Sikhs press on, silencing one pillbox after another.

At Mile 16 when the tanks don't show up till 8.20 p.m., Lt Col Anant Singh talks to his Adjutant Capt S.S. Duggal on the radio set. 'Bhaiband or no bhaiband, every jawan of 4 Sikh is a bhaiband. Tell them to move,' he says. Lt Kanwaljit Singh is tuned on the same frequency. He knows the code word for tanks is bhaiband or brother. 'Before Duggal could speak to me, I was on the move,' he says. Immediately to the left of the road, in line with Barki, is a police station. Delta Company targets that. Twenty minutes after the attack, the Shermans show up and start firing. The troops in the tanks do not know that the attack has already been launched and in the dark of the night they fire at Barki not realizing that they are hitting their own men. A horrified Lt Kanwaljit Singh runs to the closest tank with his signaller following, when the man's arm is blown off in the tank fire. He tries to locate the telephone on the vehicle for Infantry tank conversation but cannot find it. He climbs the tank and bangs on its cupola with his Sten gun. A Dafadar comes out. Lt Kanwaljit Singh tells him to stop firing along the road and on its right since the attack is already under way. The message is passed on to the other tanks and the fire is directed to the left of the road. Delta Company moves ahead and captures the police station and finds a small drain in front, which they later use as a trench.

Continuous fire coming from Barki makes the advance difficult. The battalion mortars are now directed at the village. While the artillery fires on the enemy, 4 Sikh moves its own machine guns forward to engage enemy machine guns in the pillboxes. Thus, the assaulting companies move forward in short spurts by fire-and-move tactics. They close in on the objective, refusing to be halted by enemy bullets. Casualties during the assault are left unattended because every minute counts. The last 90 metres to Barki prove to be the most difficult. However, the sight of the Sikhs advancing towards them has a demoralizing effect on the Pakistanis and their resistance suddenly disintegrates. At 9.10 p.m., after an hour of gruesome battle, the guns fall silent. All that can now be seen in Barki is smoke rising from burning vehicles and bunkers. Mingled with the whisper of the wind is the Sikh battle cry, *'Bole so nihal, sat sri akal'* which echoes in the battlefield amidst the moans of pain of the injured, lying soaked in their own blood. Two flares then screech across the sky. Those who see them rejoice. They signal that Barki has been won.

Yet another brave

The Battle of Barki was a testament to the bravery of the 4 Sikh. But an incident that took place after the war showed just how brave a lady married to one of its officers was. Though she did not go to the battlefield to fight, her act of courage is no less than that of the men who did.

While Sub Ajit Singh got a Maha Vir Chakra in the Battle of Barki, there was another Ajit Singh posted into 4 Sikh just before it went to war. He was 2Lt Ajit Singh. When 4 Sikh was moving to Ferozepur by a special train, it made a halt at Meerut, which used to be the Sikh Regimental Centre in those days. There, at the station, they were met by the Centre Commandant and some young officers who brought lunch for the famished men. Amongst the officers was a young Sikh—2Lt Ajit Singh—who had been posted to 4 Sikh but was scheduled to be sent later. When he came to know that the battalion was going to war, 2Lt Ajit volunteered to go early. He was keen to fight the war and had asked the regimental centre to send him to the battalion as soon as possible. 'He came to us on 2 September, when we were in the thick of battle, and was posted to Charlie Company,' remembers Brig Kanwaljit Singh (Retd). Since everyone was busy with the war, young Ajit was not given any responsibilities. However, he was so motivated that he insisted on accompanying the battalion wherever it went and tried to help in whatever way he could. After the capture of Barki, he accompanied the battalion to Khem Karan, where he died in artillery shelling. And thus ended the brief career of an enthusiastic and highly motivated young officer.

After repatriation of the prisoners of war, when officers from 4 Sikh reached Mathura, a young girl came to meet them. She wanted to know about Ajit. She was his wife and was expecting his baby. She had been told earlier that he had died in enemy shelling, and had even been handed over the *kada* he used to wear, but she still nursed a faint hope that he might be alive. 'When we told her that it was not so, she said that it was her husband's dream to serve with 4 Sikh. He could not do it for long but she vowed that if she had a son, she would send him to 4 Sikh,' remembers Brig Singh. As destiny would have it, she did have a son. On 8 June 1985, 2Lt Satpreet Singh, son of late 2Lt Ajit Singh, reported to 4 Sikh on his first posting, two decades after his father had joined it. Col Satpreet Singh is still serving in the Army.

Some mishaps

There were some unfortunate occurrences that night. Brig Singh remembers that just after his company captured the police station, he was startled to hear a loud bang behind him. 'I turned around to find that one of our tanks had blown up on a mine,' he says. They then realized that before deserting Barki, the enemy soldiers had scattered anti-tank mines on both sides of the road. They had not had time to cover these and the mines could be seen throughout the route, but because it was dark, the tanks were in danger of moving over them and getting blown up. 'I was under the impression that armoured guys only spoke English, so I immediately looked for someone in my company who had a working knowledge of English. Hav Mahender Singh, a towering Sikh basketball player, who had cleared his matric exam and could speak in broken English, caught my eye. I told him to go back and inform the tanks that Barki had been captured so there was no need to fire. I also told him to warn them not to go off the road as mines had been planted there.' The tanks stopped after that. However, within minutes, an RCL jeep came speeding in Lt Kanwaljit Singh's direction. It screeched to a halt just right of him, reversed and went over a mine, exploding in front of his eyes. It was the Commandant of Central India Horse, Lt Col S.C. Joshi, who had borrowed a 4 Sikh jeep and had come to assess the situation. He was evacuated but could not be saved.

After capturing Barki, Alpha and Charlie companies could see the eastern bank of Ichhogil Canal and, in the adrenaline rush of the victory, they went right across and took over that bank as well. A patrol from Delta Company was also sent with them but Sub Massa Singh, who was leading it, got caught in machine-gun fire and succumbed to his injuries. The Pakistanis had fled from Barki and regrouped on the other bank of the canal, from where they were firing at the Indians. The canal itself was a formidable obstacle—140 ft wide and 30 ft deep with about 20 ft of water. The bank was 3 ft higher on Pakistan's side and also had pillboxes. The 4 Sikh soldiers could see the turrets and guns of tanks that were moving behind that embankment and bringing devastating fire in their wake.

16 Punjab swings into action

Once Barki had been captured, it was time for 16 Punjab to move in and capture the area further north. They ran into two pillboxes from where the Pakistanis were still firing. One of these was disabled by Sepoy Balam Ram who crawled up to the pillbox undetected by the Pakistanis. Putting his own life at risk, he stood up and, in one swift move, pushed aside the barrel of a machine gun that had been firing from one of the openings to lob in a grenade. A blast rent the air and the pillbox was silenced. Balam Ram was later decorated with a Vir Chakra and retired as a Havildar. The second pillbox was neutralized by 2Lt R. Vijay Rajan. The twenty-year-old officer took a section of men and slowly sneaked up behind the bunker. The men smashed the door open from the back and rushed in, overpowering the Pakistanis. They managed to capture a Pakistani Junior Commissioned Officer and two soldiers.

Led by Maj Ranjit Singh, 16 Punjab's Delta Company launched an attack on the northern side of the bridge and secured the canal bank. Bravo Company, led by Lt Manmohan Singh, attacked the southern side of the canal. Thereafter, the plan was for Alpha Company, led by Lt V.P. Gaba, to cross over to the other side to establish a bridgehead and the engineers were ready to blow up the bridge after they had done it. Survivors from Alpha Company were to then swim across the canal that was overflowing with water, with the help of ropes, bringing back injured men if they could. However, the same afternoon, Pakistan destroyed the bridge on their own thus completing the job for 16 Punjab. Lt Col J.S. Bhullar, 16 Punjab Commanding Officer, also gave a victory signal.

Aren't you fed up with the war?

Col Manmohan Singh recounts an amusing story from the battle. After ceasefire had been declared, Barki was placed under the supervision of United Nations (UN) observers. On the night of 24 September when he sent his men on a routine patrol they found that a Pakistani section led by a Havildar had crossed the Cease-Fire Line. 'The next morning we went to them waving white flags,' he says. 'I told them they had come into our side and should withdraw, otherwise we would be forced to attack them.' The Pakistani Havildar looked scared, but said he was helpless since he had been ordered to cross the Cease-Fire Line. 'I told him he would be killed, to which he shrugged his shoulders and answered, "*Agar kismet mein yehi likha hoga to yehi hoga, sahab* (Whatever is destined will happen)."' Around 5 p.m., Lt Manmohan Singh was directing 3-inch mortar fire on the invaders when a soldier told him that a UN observers' jeep seemed to be headed that way. When he asked his Commanding Officer what he should do, he was told not to let the observers come close. 'We fired an RCL round near their jeep, making sure we did not hit them,' he recounts. The UN observers stepped out of the jeep and disappeared into the fields. Lt Manmohan Singh and his men happily got back to firing their mortars at the Pakistanis. Soon he felt a tap on his shoulder. It was one of the UN observers standing right behind him. 'Hey Captain, aren't you fed up with the war?' he asked. A sheepish Lt Manmohan Singh then explained to him how the Pakistani section had invaded the Indian side. When they checked after the firing, the Pakistanis had returned to their own side.

A brilliant military move

The capture of Barki is considered a brilliant military move that was executed by 7 Infantry Division with prudence and foresight. The high casualties suffered by the participating units prove how hard the men fought to take over a heavily defended terrain. Barki was literally a fortress, defended by automatic weapons and supported by artillery and armour. Military historians believe that the performance of the Army in Barki largely compensated the reverses that had been suffered by India in the other areas.

The 16 Punjab lost twenty-one men, while fifty were wounded. They were awarded the Battle Honour Barki. Central India Horse, less two squadrons, lost six tanks during this action. The 4 Sikh suffered the highest casualties. Thirty-nine of their men, including three Junior Commissioned Officers, were killed, while as many as 120 were injured, including Maj Manhas and Capt Duggal. The gallantry awards of Maha Vir Chakra to Sub Ajit Singh (Posthumous) and Vir Chakra to Maj Shamsher

Singh Manhas, Nb/Sub Ajmer Singh and L/Nk Pritam Singh (Posthumous) enhanced the unit's Roll of Honour. The 4 Sikh was awarded with the Battle Honour Barki and the Theatre Honour Punjab. A number was not put to the enemy casualties but it is said that three truckloads of dead bodies were taken away by Pakistan. Barki was held by a platoon of 17 Punjab under Maj Raja Aziz Bhatti (Company Commander Alpha Company) reinforced with another platoon of 12 Punjab along with troops that had retreated from Hudiara. Two companies of Pakistan's 17 Punjab were also reportedly on the west bank of Ichhogil Canal and the bridge area on the eastern side. Maj Bhatti, the officer who defended Barki so valiantly, was killed in shelling a day after the Battle of Barki while he was directing fire at the Indians from a tree across Ichhogil Canal. He was awarded the Nishan-i-Haider, Pakistan's highest gallantry award.

When heroes became prisoners of war

Though 4 Sikh had done a marvellous job capturing Barki, their trial by fire was not over yet. Around 9.30 a.m. on 11 September, the morning after the battle, their Commanding Officer Lt Col Anant Singh was called to the 7 Infantry Division Headquarters. There he was given a special task in Khem Karan by Army Commander Lt Gen Harbaksh Singh, VrC, who also happened to be the Colonel of the Sikh regiment. The plan was that 4 Sikh would be taken in Army trucks and dropped at Valtoha from where they would march cross-country through 19 km of unreconnoitred terrain, infiltrate enemy lines and form a roadblock on Khem Karan–Kasur road by 5 a.m. on 12 September. At first light, 4 Mountain Division, which was already fighting in the Khem Karan area, would advance on the Valtoha–Khem Karan road, led by the tanks of 9 Horse. The Sikhs had been told that the advancing troops and tanks of 4 Mountain Division would make contact with them by 8 a.m. the next morning.

Although the battalion had suffered heavy casualties and the soldiers had been fighting for nearly seven days without much rest, Lt Col Anant Singh accepted the challenge. By 5 p.m., 4 Sikh was pulled out of Barki amidst enemy shelling. They marched to Khalra in three hours. 'We were filthy and tired, we hadn't changed our clothes for days, many of us had upset stomachs from drinking water from ponds, yet we came marching with our heads held high after the victory we had achieved,' says Brig Kanwaljit Singh (Retd). Battalion quarter master Lt P.P.S. Virk had got a hot meal prepared for the battle-weary soldiers and they ate heartily after many days. Here, around midnight, a cool and composed Lt Col Singh briefed his Company Commanders and then addressed the troops. 'God seems to be happy with 4 Sikh. He wants us to commemorate Saragarhi in real Saragarhi spirit,' he said. He implored his men to be brave, to remember the heroes of Saragarhi and make the battalion proud once again, on the same day. His troops nodded in agreement.

The Sikhs started walking from Valtoha at I a.m. on 12 September. It was Saragarhi Day and the men went in high spirits, looking forward to the encounter with the enemy despite being bone-tired. The men walked— some along the railway line, others through fields of sugar cane and cotton, and elephant grass—guided by two of their own soldiers who knew the area well. They were carrying recoilless guns as a precautionary measure just in case they ran into enemy tanks. However, the heavy load was slowing them down. Based on information they had received, enemy resistance was expected to be weak and they had been told that there was no tank threat, so Lt Col Singh finally took the decision that the guns would be sent back so that the battalion could move faster. 'We had been told to reach by 5 a.m. and we literally ran to get there in time' says Brig Singh.

In between they encountered an enemy column that was dealt with deftly and the march continued.

By 4 a.m., the Sikhs were less than a kilometre from village Khem Karan. They were shocked to find enemy tanks in large numbers. Enemy patrols simultaneously discovered the Sikhs and enemy aircraft started pounding the area. When the leading elements of 4 Mountain Division could not show up till 10.30 a.m., the Sikhs had no option but to challenge the enemy tanks and fight valiantly. Unfortunately, they were outnumbered and surrounded. Some managed to get back to a secure area but five officers, including Lt Col Anant Singh and Lt Kanwaljit Singh, four Junior Commissioned Officers and 121 Other Ranks were captured. Lt T.S. Shergill of 9 Horse, sent to link up with 4 Sikh, was also captured when all three of his tanks were blown up, though he put up a valiant fight and knocked down a few enemy tanks.

The prisoners of war were repatriated in February 1966. By that time 4 Sikh had been re-raised and sent back to Barki where it was honoured by a visit by the then President of India Sarvepalli Radhakrishnan who congratulated the battalion on its accomplishment in the battle.

. . .

When SUB AJIT SINGH reaches the enemy pillbox,
a burst of medium machine-gun fire immediately hits him
in the chest. He collapses; though his vision is blurring
and his body is refusing to obey his command, he pulls
out a grenade. Staggering up to the pillbox, he pushes
aside the smoking barrel of a machine gun and lobs the
grenade inside. '*Bole so nihal, sat sri akal,*' he whispers and falls
as the grenade bursts inside.

Sub Ajit Singh

Maha Vir Chakra

6 September 1965

The Sikh soldier shifts his weight from one foot to the other. Of medium height, he is well built and sinewy. His fitness comes from Army training and from sweating it out on the sports field. Sub Ajit Singh is his battalion's best hockey player. His skin is the colour of ripened wheat—the same wheat that used to grow in rich golden tufts back home in Subhana village. Hidden in the sugar cane fields, he is watching the pillbox up ahead, from where devastating fire is coming at his men. There is sweat on his brow and frustration in his large, long-lashed eyes that are tinged with red. He is holding his rifle in his hands but knows it is useless before the bunker that is spewing death on his men. Made of concrete and steel, it is like a closed room with thick walls and a roof. The walls have loopholes through which the guns are being fired. From the fire coming at him, he can make out that there have to be at least one medium machine gun and one light machine gun inside. He can also hear the deadly hiss of a Sten gun. He can't see the enemy but since there are three weapons firing at the same time, there have to be at least three Pakistani soldiers manning the pillbox, he deduces. The pillbox has to be neutralized. Bravo Company has been given the task of capturing the border outpost Rakh Hardit Singh. The only way to do it seems to be to get inside and kill the men. But how? There has to be a door from where the men get in, he reasons, but it is probably at the back. All he can see is a wall of fire, blocking the way for his men. He mouths an expletive in Punjabi and wipes the sweat off his brow. CO sahab's words ring in his ears. He had spoken to the men at the Battalion Gurudwara Sahab just before they left Ferozepur to go to war. It was an emotional speech that touched the men to the core. 'We are fortunate to have got an opportunity to go back to claim the homes we were thrown out of by the Pakistanis,' Lt Col Anant Singh had said. 'Sacrifices will have to be made but these will not go to waste. We will come back with achievements. Be fearless. Remember our gurus, remember the heroes of Saragarhi. Victory shall be ours.'

Ajit is seething in angry frustration. There is no way to get to Barki without silencing that pillbox. A shadow falls over his dark moist eyes. He wipes an angry tear and decides he will not wait any longer. *'Wahe guruji da khalsa, wahe guruji di fateh,'* he whispers to himself. Adrenaline courses wildly through his veins. Even as his comrades watch in disbelief, he starts crawling towards the bunker, right into the wall of fire.

'Ajit Singh was one of our finest Junior Commissioned Officers,' recalls Col Baldev Singh Chahal (Retd). Col Chahal knew Sub Ajit Singh well, as he was the Captain of the 4 Sikh hockey team in which he used to play. 'He was a skilled hockey player and had played for the Sikh Regimental Centre team at the command level. He was also our training Junior Commissioned Officer (JCO), polite, well mannered and very compassionate to the men,' Col Chahal says, mentioning one particular hockey match in which he had played. 'It was a match we had with the Brigade. We were losing by one goal. At half-time, I drew the men together and told them we had to score that goal. It was a question of the unit's *izzat* [honour]. Ajit was charged up. He goaded and encouraged the boys and though he used to play as a defender, he performed exceptionally well with a do-or-die spirit, filling the others with enthusiasm, and ensured that the goal was scored.'

It was the same spirit that Sub Ajit Singh displayed in war during one of the first operations of 4 Sikh in the Battle of Barki. He put his life at stake for the izzat of his battalion. It was thanks to his efforts that the border outpost Rakh Hardit Singh could be captured.

Sub Gurdev Singh, the then senior JCO of B Company, fondly remembers Ajit as a go-getter who was ready to take on any challenge that came his way. He attributes this to Ajit's sportsman spirit, which did not allow him to give up. Each time he fell, he would get up, raring to go. His company had seen him display this virtue on the hockey field, and they saw it again on the battlefield of Barki. The other quality Sub Gurdev Singh remembers about Ajit is that he was completely fearless. His bold and confrontational outlook instilled courage in the younger boys of the battalion. His bravery was contagious and helped his company face the enemy boldly. He set a personal example of how a soldier could fight and die for the honour of his battalion and his country.

Sub Ajit Singh has reached the bunker, miraculously unhurt. Since he has crawled really low, unmindful of the nettles and stones ripping his clothes and cutting into his skin, most of the fire has passed above his head, its heat singeing his turban. When the bursts come, he lowers his head and buries his nose in the ground, his rifle pressing against his side, the grenades on his belt digging into his waist. It is these grenades that give him an idea. When he reaches the pillbox, he stands up straight, with complete disregard for his life. A burst of medium machine-gun fire hits him almost immediately in the chest, pushing him down with its impact. He staggers and collapses, but as a sportsman he is used to getting up after each fall. He lifts his hand to touch his chest and it feels wet and warm. In the glow of the rising sun, he looks at his hand. It is stained with blood. With a grimace, he wipes it on his trousers.

The pain is wracking his brain; he knows he doesn't have much time. Gasping for breath, he coughs out blood and then stands up again, for the very last time. Reaching for a grenade on his belt, he pulls it out. Though his vision is blurring and his body is refusing to obey his command, he wills his mouth to locate the pin. Holding it firmly between his teeth, he pulls it out. Staggering up to the wall of the pillbox, he pushes aside the smoking barrel of a machine gun and lobs the grenade inside. *'Bole so nihal, sat sri akal,'* he whispers and falls even as the grenade bursts inside. Screams of terror from the enemy soldiers rent the air as Sub Ajit Singh tumbles to the ground and his eyes close.

When the plume of smoke lifts around the targeted pillbox, the machine guns are silent. The men who have watched Ajit perform this act of furious bravery, rush in. They kick open the door and storm the pillbox. They find three Pakistani soldiers lying there dead. Ajit, the finest hockey player of the battalion, is found outside the pillbox, his blood seeping into the land his ancestors had been forced to leave eighteen years ago. His gun is lying by his side. He has succumbed to his injuries.

For the supreme courage and devotion to duty that he displayed, Sub Ajit Singh is later decorated with the Maha Vir Chakra, the second highest gallantry award of independent India.

Sub Ajit Singh, MVC, was the son of Lance Havildar Clerk Ujagar Singh who was also from 4 Sikh. His mother was Prakash Kaur. He was born on 1 January 1933. He belonged to Subhana village, 12 km from Jalandhar. He was enrolled in the Army on 23 May 1952 and sent to 4 Sikh, an Infantry battalion with a proud history. A few years later, his younger brother too joined the same battalion. Little did anyone know that Ajit would bring more glory to it. On 6 September 1965, he was killed in the Battle of Barki. He was thirty-two years old and was survived by his wife and two daughters. His brother, who was also fighting in Barki, was sent home on early retirement since there were no male members left to look after the family. Ajit's wife is no more; their daughters are now married. His brother still lives in the village with his two sons.

The Battle of Dograi

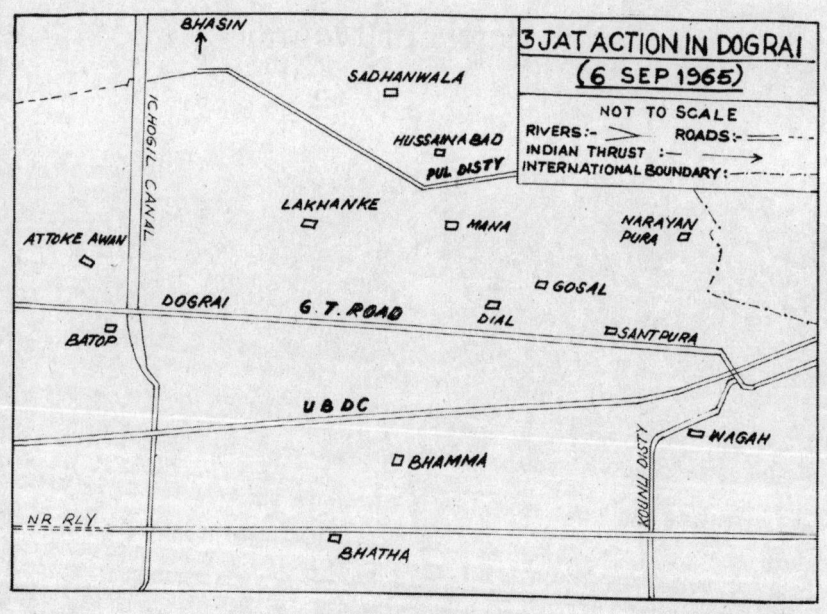

Courtesy: History Division, Ministry of Defence

On 1 September 1965, soon after Pakistan's Operation Gibraltar to take over Kashmir failed and India advanced 8 km into Pakistan-occupied Kashmir to capture Haji Pir Pass, Pakistan launched a counter-attack. It was called Operation Grand Slam and was aimed at occupying the important town of Akhnoor in Jammu and Kashmir. Pakistan's aim was to cut off communication and supply routes to Indian troops. Attacking with a large force of troops and Pattons that were technically superior to India's tanks, Pakistan took the Indian Army by surprise and inflicted heavy losses. India responded by calling in the Air Force. However, the very next day, the Pakistan Air Force attacked Indian forces and airbases in both Kashmir and Punjab.

India then decided to shift the theatre of war to Pakistan's Punjab area. The aim was to attack from the west so that the enemy would be forced to relocate troops engaged in the Akhnoor operation to defend Punjab. The 54 Infantry Brigade planned this using the units 15 Dogra, 13 Punjab, C Squadron of 14 Horse and 3 Jat. This move proved to be the turning point of the war. Commanded by Lt Col Desmond E. Hayde, 3 Jat made history in that war in spite of the fact that it had been given a subsidiary role as it had moved into the area only recently. It was also logistically ill-prepared for the war. Having arrived from the Eastern Sector, the battalion did not have any recoilless anti-tank guns till the end of August; no one in the battalion had fired those weapons in the past four years. Also, battalion mortars and medium machine guns were unfamiliar weapons for the troops. To add to all this, the battalion did not have a full strength of soldiers; they were short by nearly a hundred (equivalent to one rifle company).

Disregarding the handicaps, the battalion started its advance towards Ichhogil Canal (which marked the de facto border between the two countries) at 9 a.m. on 6 September. The Pakistan Army held the bridges over the canal and blew up those it could not hold, thus closing routes towards Lahore. A fierce battle raged on the banks of the canal. The heavy weapons component of 3 Jat was destroyed by the Pakistani air attack and they were unable to communicate with the Brigade headquarters. Till 3.15 p.m. the Jats faced intensive attack and shelling but stoically kept clearing Pakistanis from the east bank of the canal, eventually going on to capture the town of Dograi. At 11.10 a.m., they cleared the massive Batapore shoe factory on the west bank of the canal. Unfortunately, higher commanders had no information of these victories; misinformation led to the battalion being ordered to withdraw from Batapore and Dograi. The Jats moved back about 9 km to a place called Santpura where they dug trenches and held fast despite enemy efforts to dislodge them. Pakistan turned Dograi into a virtual fortress. There was a massive ingress of enemy troops, mortars and machine guns.

On the night of 21 September, 3 Jat attacked Dograi once again and recaptured it, though this time both sides suffered heavy casualties. It was an infantry battle of such great proportions that it is regarded as an epic and is now part of military history lessons. For the daring second assault on Dograi and its fearless capture, 3 Jat was awarded the Battle Honour Dograi. For the first attack and capture of Dograi, Lt Col Hayde, Commanding Officer (CO), was awarded the Maha Vir Chakra. The battalion's exemplary performance is considered to be the result of Lt Col Hayde's great personal courage and exceptional qualities of leadership.

I heard the gritty story of the Battle of Dograi from Maj Gen B.R. Varma, AVSM, who was Capt Varma—Battalion Adjutant—in 1965 and Col Durjan Singh Shekhawat (Retd), who was Maj Shekhawat—battalion 2IC—then. Though I had met and spent a lot of time talking to Brig Hayde in Delhi's Army Research and Referral Hospital during his last days there, I had no idea then that I would be writing about the Battle of Dograi or that he wasn't going to be around for much longer. By the time the Army approached me to write this book, Brig Hayde had already passed on. Here is the story of Dograi as seen through the eyes of the two brave soldiers who survived the war and returned to tell the tale.

The night of 21–22 September, 1965

In the purple sky a Very light shines. Like a flash of daylight it traces an arc and illuminates the wheat fields. There is a faint rustle in the short dry stumps of the harvested crop as a slight breeze picks up, but there is hardly any other movement. From their cemented pillboxes, the soldiers of

Pakistan's 16 Punjab (Pathan) watch, rifles cocked, machine guns spouting smoke. They know the Indians are out there in the darkness somewhere and they are trying to find out where. That is why they are on high alert; their artillery guns are blazing and their deadly fire is raining down on Grand Trunk Road from where they are expecting the Indian Army to strike.

Just 700-odd metres away, on a tangent to Grand Trunk Road—from where the Pakistanis least expect a strike— stand the Jats, watching quietly. All attack companies have walked 9 km from Santpura, where they were holed up for almost two weeks, and have reached the Forming Up Places (FUP). Though the night is brilliantly lit by exploding shells and tracer bullets, the soldiers are in the shadows. The sound of gunfire is interrupted only by the call of crickets and the tread of boots as the four companies (550 men, most of them tall and sturdy Jats) briskly move on. Each of them is holding a 7.62-rifle with 200 rounds, with at least two grenades hanging off the belt pouch. On each man's hip hangs his water bottle on the right and bayonet on the left. They expect hand-to-hand fighting and know that they might have to fix bayonets on their rifles for the final assault. 'It was a pitch-dark night but we didn't need lights to locate Dograi,' remembers Gen Varma. There were two reasons for this, he explains. The first was that during the two weeks they had spent in the trenches at Santpura, they had done so many reconnaissance trips of the area that each soldier was familiar with almost every bush around Dograi. The second reason was that Dograi was so brightly lit that it appeared to be on fire. 'So much artillery fire was coming from there and being returned from the Indian side that we could see it in silhouette, bathed in an orange glow.'

At 1.30 a.m., they break into a brisk walk, rifles trained. Ten minutes later, they enter Dograi. There is so much noise already that they don't bother about keeping it quiet. Loud war cries of '*Jat Balwan, Jai Bhagwan*' fall into the ears of the waiting Pakistanis. Machine-gun fire rings out. The battle has begun.

REMEMBERING DOGRAI

Kahe sune ki baat na bolun, gaaun dekhi bhai; Teen Jat ki katha sunaun, sun le mere bhai;
Ikkis sitambar raat ghaneri, hamla jaaton ne mari, dushman mein mach gayi khalbali, kaanp uthi Dograi

(What I speak of is not hearsay, I've seen it with my own eyes; this is the story of 3 Jat, listen carefully, my brother. On 21 September, the night was pitch-dark when the Jats attacked Dograi, so fierce was the fight that enemy soldiers ran amok in terror and Dograi trembled)

—Col Harendra Kumar Jha

These lines are from a popular Haryanvi song commemorating the Battle of Dograi. They best describe one of the most famous battles of the 1965 war that saw eighty-one fatal casualties in India's 3 Jat and around 300 in Pakistan's 16 Punjab in a hand-to-hand fight that raged through the night but was at its most brutal for just about an hour.

Meeting the two veterans

Something I have learnt in the course of writing two war books is that battles leave behind scars. These could be on a soldier's psyche or his body, or they could be scars of the worst kind—left behind in hearts that have lost people they loved.

This belief gets reinforced when, on a sweltering May morning, Maj Gen B.R. Varma (Retd), AVSM, opens the gates of his tree-shaded Gurgaon bungalow to me at 10.30 a.m. sharp. He walks briskly, but with a pronounced limp. He notes that I have noticed it and smiles. 'The Battle of Dograi took an inch and a half off my leg. I got two bullets,' he says. I just nod politely. I am getting used to war injuries. I am also getting used to the grace with which soldiers accept and live with them. From Maj Gen Varma I hear the first part of the story of the Battle of Dograi. The second part of the story (picking up from where Maj Gen Varma sustained the bullet injuries and was evacuated) comes from Col Durjan Singh Shekhawat (Retd), AVSM, who was battalion 2IC during the war.

Col Shekhawat is eighty-four. He lives in Jaipur though he no longer sports the big bushy Rajput moustache that once made enemy soldiers say, '*Wahan badi muchhon wala Hindustani Major baitha hai.*' Neither is his memory what it used to be—he fumbles for dates and names, apologetically telling me that age has caught up with him. However, he still insists that he will come and pick me up from Jaipur Railway Station. Later, sipping on a glass of chilled *nimbu pani*, he stifles a smile when he recounts how he badgered his Brigade Commander and arm-twisted his course mate in the

Military Secretary branch (from where Army officers get their postings) into sending him back to his battalion the moment he came to know that it was going to war.

'I couldn't bear the thought that while I was posted in Siliguri, my battalion was going to face action in Punjab. I told my Brigade Commander that my fifteen years of service would be wasted if I didn't get a chance to fight in the war. Finally, he wished me luck and let me go,' he recalls.

Col Shekhawat (who was thirty-five-year-old Maj Shekhawat then) quickly tossed his toothbrush and uniforms into his backpack, and caught the first train to Punjab. He then boarded a bus that took him halfway to his destination. He waited on the highway and thumbed a ride on a passing truck, and finally hitch-hiked his way to Santpura where his comrades were camping in trenches. He was immediately appointed battalion 2IC. Though he had missed the first attack on Dograi, Shekhawat reached just in time for the second attack.

Gen B.R. Varma's story

The date was 6 September 1965. Restless butterflies were fluttering in twenty-five-year-old Capt B.R. Varma's stomach as he listened to the radio. He was getting married in two days' time and even though he didn't want to admit it, he was a bit nervous. This was his second attempt at marrying the same girl. Earlier that year, his marriage had been fixed for 15 April, but due to the escalating tension between India and Pakistan and war predictions, his leave had suddenly been cancelled. Now another date had been set for Capt Varma's marriage.

Just then his attention was drawn to a radio announcement. War had broken out between India and Pakistan, and all soldiers on leave had been asked to rejoin their units. When Capt Varma informed his parents and the girl's family, the latter implored him to have a quick wedding ceremony before he left. The young officer refused. 'What if I don't come back from the war, I told them. They saw the logic in that and did not pressurize me further,' he remembers. The next evening, he caught the special train to Amritsar from Old Delhi Railway Station. He then hitched a ride on a three-ton truck bound for Khasa where his battalion was located, only to find that they had already crossed the International Border and moved ahead on 6 September. He finally joined them at Santpura, about 3 km ahead of the Wagah border.

Surviving Pak shelling

Capt Varma was welcomed with open arms by his men and Lt Col Hayde immediately appointed him as Battalion Adjutant. While at Santpura, 3 Jat spent all its time preparing for the battle that they knew was to follow. There was no doubt in anyone's mind that Dograi would be captured. They had done it once and they would do it again. They would go on day as well as night patrols to familiarize themselves with the area and the objectives. Every day, they faced the wrath of Pakistani firepower; it became a routine affair and they were left unimpressed by it. Maj Gen Varma recounts how the CO helped create a sense of couldn't-care-less nonchalance. 'All of us were in trenches dug out at Santpura. The CO would be sitting inside with his legs propped up against the side wall.

The moment the Pakistanis started shelling the area, he would strap on his helmet and jump out of the trench, walking calmly through the enemy fire. That was his way of showing his men that they had nothing to fear. He would say, "Only a bullet that is meant for me can kill me. I don't need to fear the rest." This spirit of confident fearlessness was conveyed to the troops and they too started taking the shelling in their stride.' The weeks preceding 21 September had been of such intense battle preparation for the Jats that they were at a psychological peak when the time came to launch an attack. They had done so much patrolling and preliminary preparation that not one man felt they would not succeed in capturing Dograi. When the final battle call came, they were raring to go and get it over with once and for all.

The plan

The attack plan is typical of Lt Col Hayde—clear, concise and daring. All rifle companies are to be sent simultaneously in a deliberate attack through the FUP. They have been given clear objectives—occupation of various parts of Dograi. The orders given to the troops are crystal clear: Follow your leader who will take you straight to your objective; make your firing position immediately; do not move and shoot at anything else that moves.

'Not one man will turn back'

When he gives his men final attack orders on the night of 21 September, Lt Col Hayde makes only two demands from them. The first is: 'Ek bhi aadmi pichhe nahin hatega (Not a single man will turn back).' The second: *'Zinda ya murda, Dograi mein milna hai* (Dead or alive, we have to meet in Dograi).' He warns them against retreating from battle. 'Even if all of you run away, I shall continue to stand on the battlefield alone,' he says. 'When you go back to your village, people will spit on you for having deserted your CO in war.'

Accompanied by his 2IC, Maj Shekhawat, Lt Col Hayde goes from trench to trench after the jawans finish their dinner on the night of the attack. He speaks to them of the great glory the battle will bring them, their families and their battalion. 'If we die tonight, it will be a glorious death. Our families will be looked after by the battalion, so we have nothing to worry about,' he says, making them promise that the next day they will all meet in Dograi, whether dead or alive. The men were full of *josh*, remembers Col Shekhawat. So much so that when Lt Col Hayde confronted a soldier with '*Kal kahan milna hai?* (Where do we have to meet tomorrow?)' the soldier replied, *'Dograi mein* (In Dograi).' Stifling a smile, Lt Col Hayde (who had picked up a smattering of Jat and liked to address the soldiers as *susre*) then asks, '*Susre, agar CO sahab zakhmi ho gaya toh kya karoge?* (What will you do if your CO is wounded in war?)' The soldier replies, *'CO sahab ko uthakar Dograi mein le jaayenge kyunki susre CO sahab ke orders saaf hain—"Zinda ya murda, Dograi mein milna hai"* (We will pick up CO sahab and carry him to Dograi since his orders are clear—"Dead or alive, we have to meet in Dograi").' A thoroughly pleased Lt Col Hayde moves on to the next trench.

A little later, the officers sit down for dinner outside their bunkers, and then troop into the Adjutant's bunker awaiting final orders. Lt Jabar Singh, one of the youngest officers in the battalion, is a little nervous. He asks Maj Shekhawat, 'Sir, what is going to happen tonight?' Maj Shekhawat answers, 'We are twenty-four officers having dinner together. Some of us will not be there tomorrow. Who these officers are only God knows, but battles are not won without sacrifice.' Lt Jabar Singh listens quietly. He doesn't know then that he is one of the officers who will not be there tomorrow.

Soon after last light, the men lace up their boots, strap on their battle helmets and get ready to march forward. They reach the FUP around 1.30 a.m. Up ahead they see Dograi lit up by gunfire as if on a Diwali night. The 54 Infantry Brigade has planned the attack in two phases. The 13 Punjab has been told to overrun enemy defences east of Dograi astride Mile 13 on Grand Trunk Road in the first phase. Once Mile 13 is secured, 3 Jat is to attack and capture Dograi in the second phase. On 17 September, when the attack was being discussed, Lt Col Hayde had told the Brigade Commander, 'Regardless of phase one, 3 Jat will go through with phase two, that is, the attack.' Phase one fails. The troops of 13 Punjab are unable to secure Mile 13. The Brigade Commander informs Lt Col Hayde about this over the wireless and asks 3 Jat to call off their attack that night. Lt Col Hayde who has already reached the FUP refuses to consider it. 'We carry on. In fact, we are already at it,' he tells his Brigade Commander and then joins his rifle companies for the final assault on a blazing Dograi.

The attack

It is 1.40 a.m. when Delta, the first attacking company, hits Dograi, guns blazing. To its right is Charlie Company and to its left Bravo company. The CO's party is somewhere in between along with Battalion Headquarters and a section of Alpha Company. All companies have been told to hit different predefined objectives at the same time, not giving the enemy time to react. The approach is obstructed by minefields; machine-gun bullets fly through the air and soldiers of Pakistan's 16 Punjab (Pathan) wait for them hidden in the darkness in unknown lanes and gullies, training their guns from the windows of dilapidated huts and houses.

Quite suddenly, the Jats are stalled by a burst of fire from the right. From a cemented pillbox at the entrance of Dograi which is strongly defended, a blast of machine-gun fire hits them. No less than eight heavy and light automatics are positioned over a 180-metre area. These deadly guns are spewing fire.

While the rest watch stunned, attack halted, a confident command pierces the air. '*Sab jawan dahine taraf se mere saath, CHARGE!* (All soldiers from the right, with me. Charge!)' It is Sub Pale Ram, recipient of the Military Medal and Mention-in-Despatches award three times. His voice soars above the din like an eagle. He has taken complete command of the situation. Without looking back to see if anyone is following, Sub Pale Ram charges at the machine guns. He is unhesitatingly followed by the right-hand platoons of Charlie Company. The depth platoon of Delta Company under Capt Kapil Singh Thapa also charges. Stifling all self-preservation instincts, the Jats rush into that wall of machine-gun fire, blotting out its blaze for the ones behind. Those who fall are left by the wayside; others carry on the attack.

Sub Pale Ram takes six bullets in his chest and stomach, yet pushes himself forward, carrying his company with him. The men continue to fight till they silence the guns. Sub Pale Ram is found atop the enemy bunkers, eyes still open, breath coming in short gasps. As unbelievable as the death-defying charge he leads is the fact that he survives to tell the tale and show people the scars on his bullet-riddled body. He is later awarded the Vir Chakra. Everyone is not as lucky, however. Out of that glorious charge of 108, only twenty-seven emerge alive. 'It was an unbelievable assault. A supreme honour for anyone able to witness it,' Lt Col Hayde later writes in his book, *The Battle of Dograi*.

Capt Varma is about 18 metres behind his CO. He suddenly feels bullets piercing his right thigh and drops to the ground. The soldiers around him pick him up and try to make him stand but he collapses again. That is when they notice his ripped trousers and blood oozing through the fabric. They carry him in a foreman's lift and he limps along with them. Since the battle has just begun, they drag him into a small hut and leave him there with his weapon, while they rejoin their comrades in the attack. Sheer courage carries them across the minefields, a deep sense of loyalty keeps them going even as friends are blown to bits before their eyes. The fury that rages through their veins is stronger than the pain they endure. Men walk on with bullet-riddled bodies, using their weapons till the very last shred of strength leaves them, when, clutching their bayonet-ripped stomachs with bloodstained hands, they sink softly to the ground. As they fall, others take their place—unperturbed, satisfied with the honour that death in war brings. This is a battle they have come to win. Only one thought is stamped on their collective minds, '*Zinda ya murda, Dograi mein milna hai.*'

The battle rages through the night. It is fierce and relentless. The east bank of Ichhogil Canal comes alive with gunfire and the loud battle cries of the warriors on both sides. The enemy being attacked is equally strong if not stronger, and they are defending a robust, well-built township. A single battalion attacking and annihilating another battalion, which is supported by an additional battalion on the flanks, is a feat unheard of. But then, many unbelievable stories unfold that night.

Delta Company's Kapil Singh Thapa, a young Captain in his early twenties, has been given the task of capturing the north-eastern edge of Dograi village. Supporting the assault led by Sub Pale Ram, he bravely attacks the enemy position. A hand-to-hand fight follows. Capt Thapa launches grenades at the enemy position and gets into a bayonet fight. When he is sitting down to change his magazine, two enemy bullets rip through his helmet and into his head. The quiet Captain, a shy man of great determination but few words, closes his eyes, never to speak again. He is posthumously awarded the Maha Vir Chakra.

Meanwhile, Alpha Company reaches its objective. Company Commander Maj Asa Ram Tyagi, newly married, is hit by two bullets on his side but ignores it and continues to lead his men. They take the enemy tank crew by surprise. Two tanks are captured intact. A few days earlier, Maj Tyagi had been pulled up by Maj Shekhawat and told that the CO was not happy with his company as they had opened fire one night without any reason. This had upset Maj Tyagi quite a bit. 'Sir, let the time come, you will not find Alpha Company or Maj Tyagi wanting. We will not disappoint you,' he had said, growing emotional. He proves it that night. In the severe hand-to-hand fight that ensues, Maj Tyagi is wounded again but continues to fight. He shoots and bayonets a Pakistani Major. He himself is shot again twice at point-blank range and brutally bayoneted. Even as he falls, clutching his badly ripped stomach, Hav Ram Singh picks up a huge stone, killing his Company Commander's assailant by smashing his head. Nb/Sub Chhotu Ram, Platoon Commander, leads the attack and captures the objective. He personally assaults an enemy tank, climbs atop it like a man possessed and drops a grenade into it, killing the crew on the spot. Inspired by his bravery, his platoon overruns the position and captures three tanks. After the objective is achieved, Maj Tyagi is taken to the Regimental Aid Post set up in a hut, where Capt S.G. Timmaraddi, the medical officer, is administering first aid to the injured. By now Maj Tyagi is slipping in and out of consciousness. Capt Varma is also carried to the same hut when the battle eases and is laid down on the ground next to Maj Tyagi. All around them are battle casualties—men who have been shot or bayoneted and are stoically awaiting their fate. Capt Varma and Maj Tyagi lie there that night listening to the battle raging outside. When the time comes to evacuate casualties, Maj Tyagi tells Capt Varma, *'Aap senior hain, pehle aap jaiye* (You are senior, please go first).' Capt Varma tells him to keep quiet and go, wishing him good luck. Maj Tyagi has lost a lot of blood and is in terrible pain. He pleads with Maj Shekhawat who is evacuating casualties to shoot him and put an end to his suffering. 'Tyagi was lying with his stomach ripped open; he was still alive, though in terrible pain,' Col Shekhawat remembers. 'He told me, "Sir, I will not survive. *Aap ek goli mar dijiye. Aapke haath se mar jana chahta hun.*"' An emotional Maj Shekhawat, who was also Maj Tyagi's first Company Commander, assures him he will survive. Maj Tyagi is the first to be evacuated. Maj Shekhawat and his men place him atop a tank carrier and secure him with ropes. 'We ran ahead of the vehicle pulling out bushes and clearing fallen debris with our bare hands; we picked up fallen poles and wires, and pushed the tank carrier on to the main road. We desperately wanted Tyagi to live,' he says. In spite of all their efforts, Maj Tyagi dies on 25 September. He is posthumously awarded the Maha Vir Chakra; Nb/Sub Chhotu Ram is awarded the Vir Chakra.

The list of heroes that night runs long. Sepoy Bohit Singh of Bravo Company is part of a machine-gun detachment. Without any concern for his safety, he recklessly rushes forward to break up a counter-attack on his company. He is killed. Even after they capture the northern edge of the town, Sepoy Lehna Singh's company comes under intense enemy shelling and machine-gun fire. Uneducated and unambitious but passionately motivated, Lehna mans a light machine gun in a position completely exposed to enemy fire and mows down sixty Pakistani soldiers and destroys four vehicles. He is later awarded the Vir Chakra. Sub Khazan Singh, VrC, participates in the attack despite a head wound sustained in the first action that has left lead embedded in his head. Wounded again on 21 September, he refuses to be evacuated till the ceasefire.

Every man who fights in Dograi that night appears possessed. Those wounded regret that they cannot participate in the battle. They refuse to be evacuated, preferring to be given first aid in the trenches from where they can hear the sounds of the battle.

Dograi is captured by 3 a.m. though sporadic firing continues. By 6.15 a.m., Indian tanks arrive and start firing at the other bank of the canal, from where Pakistan has been shelling the Jats. Pakistan's back is broken and its soldiers retreat. Supporting companies on the other side that have been cut off by the Indian occupation of Dograi look for an escape route. Those that try to flee through the village are shot by 3 Jat snipers from the rooftops; some manage to circumvent them and swim across the canal.

Pakistan tries a counter-attack. Their artillery keeps pounding Dograi incessantly till 4 a.m. on 23 September, but the Jats dig in their heels and refuse to budge. They flush out enemy soldiers hiding in huts in Dograi. Among those captured are Lt Col J.F. Golwala, Commanding Officer, 16 Punjab (Pathan), Maj Taslim Beg, Battery Commander, two more officers, five Junior Commissioned Officers and 108 soldiers of Other Ranks. Three enemy officers, five Junior Commissioned Officers and 380 soldiers are killed. Three enemy tanks and two recoilless guns are destroyed. Eight 3-inch mortars, two recoilless guns, two Sherman tanks, five jeeps and two trucks are captured. The mortars are used against the enemy when Pakistan tries a counter-attack. The Indian national flag is hoisted on Ichhogil Canal by L/Nk Om Prakash. It is a proud moment for those who survive to see it; most look on with moist eyes remembering comrades who gave their lives for the capture of Dograi.

Capt Varma's turn for evacuation comes late in the afternoon. He is piled up with other casualties in a T-16, a tank-like vehicle. 'I sat on another soldier's lap as there was no place,' he tells me. Driver Khema Ram carries sixteen of them to the Advance Dressing Station established near Santpura, where they are given first aid and then sent to Amritsar Military Hospital. From there all casualties, including those coming from Barki where too a fierce battle is raging, are evacuated to Jalandhar by a special emergency medical train.

Capt Varma is taken to the Army Base Hospital, Delhi, from where he is eventually discharged on 4 May 1966. When he walks out, he has a limp that will stay with him for life. 'On 21 May I finally got married to the girl who had been waiting for me through two cancelled weddings and one war,' Gen Varma tells me, looking at his pretty wife. 'And by sheer coincidence, you are sitting here today on our forty-ninth wedding anniversary,' he adds. The twinkle in his eye makes fifty years flash past and I see him as he once was—a young Captain with a fierce war behind him. A war that took an inch and a half off his right leg, but could not touch his spirit.

Laurels

Dograi is believed to be one of the hardest battles fought and won in the history of the Indian Army. Among the martyred soldiers were Maj R.D. Vatsa, Capt K.S. Thapa and Lt Jabar Singh. Maj A.R. Tyagi also succumbed to his injuries in hospital. The battalion holds the distinction of picking up three Maha Vir Chakras. These were awarded to Lt Col D.E. Hayde, Commanding Officer, and posthumously to Maj A.R. Tyagi and Capt K.S. Thapa. The battalion was also conferred four Vir Chakras, seven Sena Medals and twelve Mention-in-Despatches awards.

Lt Gen Harbaksh Singh, General Officer Commanding-in-Chief, Western Command, addressed the battalion after the war and said, 'You have achieved a great victory which very few battalions could have done. The whole nation is proud of 3 Jat.' That was enough to make the Jats smile.

. . .

When he gives his men final attack orders on the night of
21 September 1965, LT COL DESMOND EUGENE HAYDE
makes only two demands from them. The first is, '*Ek bhi
aadmi pichhe nahin hatega* (Not a single man will turn back).'
The second, '*Zinda ya murda, Dograi mein milna hai* (Dead or
alive, we have to meet in Dograi).'

Brig Desmond Eugene Hayde
Maha Vir Chakra

In the summer of 2013, I spent a lot of time in the Officers Ward of the Army Hospital Research and Referral, Delhi, visiting my ailing father. There, I would frequently exchange greetings with his roommate—a tall and fair officer—dignified, polite and with a pronounced British accent. It was Brig Desmond Eugene Hayde (Retd), MVC, hero of the Battle of Dograi. At eighty-seven, his melanoma had metastasized to almost all his vital organs; his heart was failing him and there were large warts on his body that he would keep covered under full-sleeved shirts and socks. But irrespective of how much pain he was in, I would always find the old man either sitting up in bed reading John Grisham or walking around the room, slowly but resolutely doing his own chores. I once watched him pack a small suitcase, refusing help from anyone around. It took him nearly forty minutes—slowly bending down to take the clothes out of his drawer, then straightening up, folding them neatly and placing them in the suitcase meticulously. He went on with his task with quiet determination, ignoring the people around who were trying to avoid looking at him. At the time, I had no idea why he had got his Maha Vir Chakra. When I asked him about the famous battle he had been part of, which is cited to young Army officers as an example of great leadership, he told me to visit him at his house in Kotdwar if I really wanted to hear the story. I promised him I would.

By the time I got down to doing it, nearly two years had passed. Brig Hayde was no more. He passed away on 25 September 2013, exactly a month after he called up his battalion Subedar Major and told him to keep the rifle loaded for a gun salute. '*Pacchis sitambar ko bandook ke chamber mein goli daal dena, sahab; main jaane wala hun* (Keep the gun loaded on the 25th of September; I am going to leave),' he had said in his clipped Hindi. Eventually, I heard the story of Dograi from officers who had fought in the war with him, and came to know him better through Col Kunwar Ajay Singh (Retd), managing director of Heritage Academy, a school Brig Hayde had started for the children of Kotdwar in the name of the Mukandi Lal Sheila Hayde Society. The society is named after the late Brigadier's departed wife, Sheila Hayde, and her father, the famous Garhwali barrister and freedom fighter Mukandi Lal.

It is June in Kotdwar, a small town in the foothills of Garhwal. There is no water in the Kho River (it disappears every summer which is why it is called Kho [lost]) but the surrounding hills are green. On a still day, you can hear the bells toll in the temple of Sidhbali across the river, but today, only a breeze rustles the leaves of the old neem branches overhead. It swishes through the mango orchard, makes the litchis ripening on a nearby tree tremble and ruffles the tails of Bazooka, Cocky, Devil, Tina, Dinky and a few more dogs of assorted shades, sizes and genetic inheritance that have parked themselves around me on the sprawling lawn of the late Brig Hayde's estate. The hero of Dograi was an animal lover and had adopted forty-five strays, informs Col Singh, while generously offering me iced tea, biscuits and his memories of the old Brigadier. 'Sir would take in any ailing stray he found near his house,' he tells me. 'People would often throw in unwanted puppies over these boundary walls and he would unquestioningly adopt them too.'

Brig Hayde succumbed to skin cancer in 2013, but his dogs and his legacy remain. He bequeathed his 20-acre estate and mango orchards to the Mukandi Lal Sheila Hayde Society which is now run by Col Singh—a Kotdwar boy who had been coached by Brig Hayde for his Officers Training Academy Services Selection Board interview many years ago—and his educationist wife, Rupamala Singh. Bharati Bhavan, a beautiful old house with sloping roofs and red brick walls where the late barrister Mukandi Lal used to live, now houses the school. Brig Hayde offered his land to the couple free of cost on the agreement that they would run a school there under the auspices of the trust. He never touched the earnings from the school and willed his property to the society before his demise.

Brig Hayde was a philanthropist though his curt mannerisms, blunt speech, caustic wit and strict insistence upon punctuality often scared people off. 'Being in the same house, I had to take an appointment to meet him,' says Col Singh with a smile. 'An 8 a.m. appointment meant 8 a.m. and not 8.01 a.m.' He had little patience with people he did not ideologically agree with and would just cut himself off from anyone he didn't like. He remembers how Brig Hayde stopped talking to him for years after he opted for Air Defence instead of the Infantry. 'In his eyes I was a shammer who had chosen the easier path,' he says, laughing. Col Singh was a schoolboy when he met Brig Hayde for the first time. Later when he came back to Kotdwar to attend college, Brig Hayde coached him for his Officers Training Academy interview. When he got through but was dilly-dallying about joining the academy, Brig Hayde turned up at his house with a suitcase, told him to pack his stuff and go join the Army. Many years later, Col Singh was to leave the Army and open a school in Kotdwar—the dream project of the retired Brigadier.

Difficult paths never daunted Brig Hayde. Neither in Dograi nor in his personal life. He would go all out for causes he believed in. He was the founder-president of the Ex Servicemen's League in Kotdwar. It used to function from his house in its early days. He bought a red Maruti van and got a clerk detailed for the league and the two of them would go from village to village tracking down retired soldiers and collecting data about them.

Under the tough exterior that he liked to project, Brig Hayde was a just and soft-hearted man. Col Singh shares an incident to illustrate this. The Brigadier was invited to Lucknow to inaugurate a bust of the late Maj Asa Ram Tyagi, MVC, who had attained martyrdom in the Battle of Dograi. He did not own a car and would always employ a local taxi driver whom he would pay even before sitting in his vehicle and then tip a few thousand rupees extra, telling him that he would also have to function as his LO (Liaison Officer) for the duration of the journey. This time too he travelled in the same taxi and stayed in an Army mess for the night. The next morning when he asked for the mess bill on his way out, the unit refused to charge him for the stay. Brig Hayde did not insist, but instead left a signed cheque of Rs 1 lakh for the unit's war widows fund.

He was very generous with causes he believed in but quite frugal when it came to himself. At heart, he was a simple man who did not believe in too many luxuries. Locals remember him washing his dogs' rugs in a canal that used to run past his land. He would also be seen up on the roof of Bharati Bhavan, often shirtless, mending leaks or hammering in nails to fix a piece of wood that had come loose. Col Singh recounts one of the last trips Brig Hayde made to Delhi in his car. 'Near Safdarjang, he developed a queasy stomach and wanted to use a restroom. I drove him to Hyatt. When he saw the opulence there, he was as impressed as a school kid. He sat down and had a coffee and some cake, and told me he never knew such grand places existed in India.'

Brig Hayde continued to live in Kotdwar after his retirement and, despite having such a sprawling bungalow at his disposal, he moved into a small two-room apartment constructed behind it, calling it 'Hayden'—Hayde's den. He spent the last years of his life there with his dogs, a mynah he had nursed back to health and squirrels that would often scurry around him, climbing in and out of his pockets looking for the crumbs he would often carry. Even as a Brigade Commander in the Army, he was known for carrying squirrels around in his pockets. He never owned a mobile phone or a computer, preferring to work on his old Facit typewriter. Though most grown-ups he interacted with were nervous around him, he was Uncle D to all the children who came to Heritage Academy and would often teach them songs, playing tunes like 'Red River Valley' on his mouth organ.

Brig Desmond Eugene Hayde (Retd), MVC, was born at Exeter, United Kingdom, on 28 November 1926 into an Anglo-Indian family of Irish lineage. He was one of three sons. His father was a farrier, specializing in shoeing horses. Theirs was a family of limited means and he never lived in luxury even later in life when he could afford it. His mother used to play the piano, which inculcated in him a love for music. Educated up to Senior Cambridge at Asansol and Bangalore, he joined the Indian Military Academy, Dehradun, on 20 January 1947 and was commissioned into the Jat Regiment on 12 September 1948.

Posted in Bareilly as a young Lieutenant, he met his would-be wife, Sheila Hayde, there. She was the daughter of the renowned Garhwali barrister and freedom fighter

Mukandi Lal of Kotdwar, Pauri Garhwal. They would see each other often as he sang in the choir and she attended church regularly. They fell in love and got married in 1955. His heroic and courageous leadership led to the historic victory of the Indian Army in the Battle of Dograi and Batapore in 1965. He has the distinction of being the only military leader to be sketched by the iconic painter M.F. Husain on the battleground. This portrait enjoys place of pride at the Jat Regimental Centre museum in Bareilly.

After his retirement in 1978, he settled in Kotdwar since he had promised his wife that he would look after her father. He dedicated his life to the people of Garhwal and tirelessly worked for the welfare of the widows of ex-servicemen. His efforts were acknowledged by the Chief Minister of Uttarakhand in 2011, who awarded him the title of 'Pride of Garhwal'. Though Brig Hayde donated all the land he inherited from his wife and father-in-law to Heritage Academy, he never interfered in the functioning of the school and its staff appointments, politely telling people who approached him for jobs or small favours that he had no say in the matters of the school. Usually he kept to himself, slept with his dogs sprawled on his bed and often cooked his own breakfast, letting his man Friday Mohan fix his lunch at 1 p.m. sharp.

He did interact effortlessly with children, though. As their Uncle D, he would spend time with them, telling them stories or teaching them songs he would play on his mouth organ. His only diktat when it came to running the school was that his dogs could not be chained—with the exception of the three biters that had a bad reputation. Despite complaints from some parents who were wary of having their children chased by the dogs that roamed free on campus, he would resolutely stick to his stand, curtly telling Col Singh, 'My dogs shall not be chained.'

Brig Hayde passed away at the age of eighty-seven. He is survived by his three sons, Walter, Michael and Norman. A brood of eleven dogs still lives in the school building—mostly unchained. When his wife passed away and was buried in a cemetery near the Jat Regimental Centre, he reserved a place for himself next to her. That is where he lies buried today, remembered as a strong and fearless leader whom his men would gladly follow anywhere. He gave the children of the school an anthem based on ideals that he always lived by: *Kadam badha ke chal, sur mila ke chal / Aandhiyon se na tu dagmaga, sach ki raahon pe chal* (Match your steps and walk, sing your song and walk / Don't let storms scare you, walk on the path of truth). It carries in the wind every morning during the school assembly and fills up the shade under the mango trees where Brig and Mrs Hayde once used to walk with buckets of manure in their hands. His legacy lives on.

The Tashkent Declaration

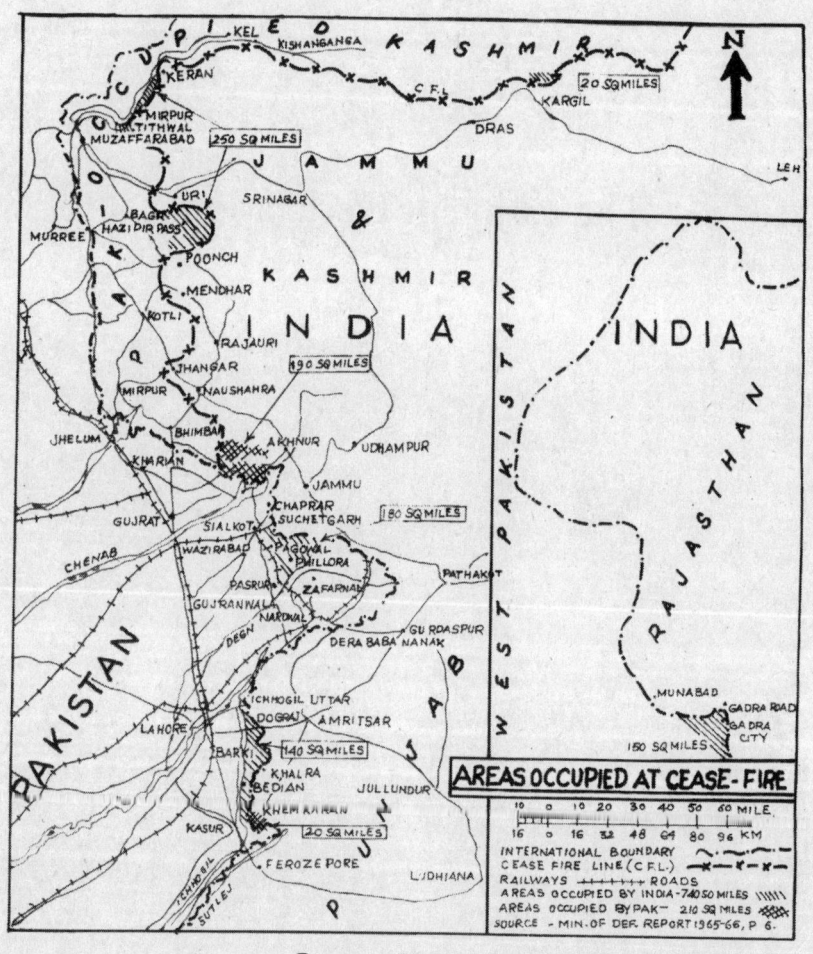

Courtesy: History Division, Ministry of Defence

The Tashkent Declaration

It is believed that India lost in Tashkent what it had gained during the war. There was a lot of unhappiness over the fact that hard-won territories had to be returned and the sacrifice of the Indian soldiers had been in vain. It is believed that Pakistan was running out of ammunition and had the war continued for a few more days, it would have broken their back. There was also the fear that the conflict might spread to other nations.

In Pakistan too there was a lot of disgruntlement. Local public opinion had been created giving the impression that they were winning the war. The signing of the declaration shocked the Pakistanis, and rioting and demonstrations erupted across the country.

The Indian Army suffered 11,479 casualties in the 1965 war (including ceasefire violations), with 2862 killed and 8617 wounded. The wounded comprised 436 officers, 347 Junior Commissioned Officers, 7768 Other Ranks and 66 Non-Combatant Enrolled employees. Pakistan says 1033 of their citizens were killed during the war. However, according to Indian records the number of Pakistanis killed stands at 5800.

On 20 September 1965, the Security Council adopted a resolution calling upon India and Pakistan to implement ceasefire on 22 September at 7 a.m. GMT (12 p.m. IST). The resolution did not satisfy either country. India had set two conditions to the ceasefire: that Pakistan would be declared the aggressor and would give an assurance that it would not interfere in Kashmir thereafter. Neither condition was agreed to. Pakistan too had hoped to defeat India with Chinese support and force plebiscite in Kashmir. This did not happen either. Within hours of an assurance to ceasefire, Pakistan's air force attacked a suburb of Amritsar, Chheratta, killing fifty-five civilians. Pakistan also made an attempt to capture maximum territory in India and fighting resumed. Ceasefire was finally declared between the two countries on 23 September at 3.30 a.m. (IST) after international pressure intensified. However, skirmishes still went on.

Starting 4 January 1966, a meeting was held in Tashkent in the Uzbek Soviet Socialist Republic (now Uzbekistan). Soviet Premier Alexei Kosygin moderated between Indian Prime Minister Lal Bahadur Shastri and Pakistani President Muhammad Ayub Khan in an attempt to create a permanent settlement. On 10 January 1966, a peace agreement was signed between the two countries. It was aimed at normalizing relations. It was agreed that both countries would pull back their armies to pre-August positions, there would be cordial exchange of prisoners of war, diplomatic and economic relations would be restored and the two countries would not interfere in each other's internal matters.

Both sides agreed to restitute territories captured in the war. Pakistani territory occupied by India during the war was approximately 1920 sq km, while Pakistan occupied about 540 sq km of Indian territory. India got back lost territories in Khem Karan and Chamb but had to return Tithwal, Haji Pir and Kargil, which were strategic areas captured at the cost of many lives. It was very difficult for Commanding Officers to explain to their soldiers why the areas captured after so much bloodshed were being returned. Col J.S. Bindra (Retd) from 1 Para, who was unit Adjutant in 1965, remembers that the soldiers had tears in their eyes as they were leaving Haji Pir. They were frustrated about having to evacuate an area they had captured after making such a valiant effort and losing so many comrades along the way.

The Tashkent Declaration was considered a big step towards establishing cordial relations between the two warring nations. However, it did nothing to limit Pakistan's guerrilla attacks in Kashmir and their interference continued. It led to another war in 1971.

At 1.30 a.m. on 11 January 1966, a few hours after signing the agreement, Prime Minister Lal Bahadur Shastri died of a heart attack. He was one of the rare Indian Prime Ministers who had boldly told the Indian Army that it could cross the border and attack Pakistan at a place of its own choosing.

The Tashkent Declaration aimed to give peace another chance in the Indian subcontinent. But the atmosphere of distrust and animosity continued. The Indo-Pak War of 1971 was just around the corner.

Acknowledgements

I would like to thank:

All the war veterans—officers and men—who dipped into their memories and helped me time travel back fifty years to the battlefields of 1965.

The Additional Directorate General of Public Information (ADGPI) for giving me this opportunity to write the amazing stories of the brave men of the Indian Army. The team ADGPI provided unstinted support and assistance in putting this project together. The editing officer of ADGPI, the book's first reader and critic, for painstakingly checking the manuscript for factual correctness.

Noted military historian and author of five books, Squadron Leader Rana Chinna (Retd), secretary of the United Service Institution of India: Centre for Armed Forces Historical Research, New Delhi, for his guidance and permission to use the library. Whenever I was plagued by doubts, not only did he make time for me and dip into his phenomenal memory for information and contacts, he also let me borrow books on his card and literally live on the USI campus while I was researching the 1965 war.

Renu Agal, my old friend, for introducing me to Penguin.

Arpita Basu, my book editor, for her tireless editing and those post-midnight and Sunday mails that assured me I was not the only one putting my life on hold to meet deadlines.

My childhood friend Renee Grewal for correcting the Punjabi used in Dfr Vir Singh's quotes and battle descriptions.

Lt Col Manoj Rawat, my husband, for dropping me off at railway stations and airports, for flexing his muscles and growling at cab drivers to ensure I got back home safely. And for (un)complainingly driving me down to destinations where none of the above wanted to go. Also for putting a pillow over his head and going off to sleep while I typed on my laptop into the wee hours.

My son, Saransh the Wise, for learning to fix his own cup noodles and salami sandwiches when I couldn't be around for him.

My mom, Sushila Bisht, for the unconditional love she has always given me and my dad, Brig B.S. Bisht, SM, VSM, for reading the 11-point-size Arial printouts, and for occasionally telling me, *'Accha likha hai. Shabaash!'*

The Battle of Haji Pir was recreated from interviews with Brig Arvinder Singh (Retd) and Col J.S. Bindra (Retd). The profile of Lt Gen R.S. Dyal, MVC, was drawn from interviews with Mrs Birender Dyal and Brig Kuldeep Singh Chandpuri, MVC.

The Battle of Asal Uttar was recreated from narratives by Lt Col H.R. Janu (Retd), SM, of 4 Grenadiers; Lt Gen Jimmy Vohra (Retd), PVSM, SM, of 9 Horse, and Lt Col Ram Prakash Joshi (Retd) of 3 Cavalry. The tank fight was recreated from an interview with Ris Maj Daya Chand Rathi (Retd), SM, from 3 Cavalry; and CQMH Abdul Hamid's profile from interviews with his wife, Rasoolan Bibi, his grandson Jameel Alam and his driver, Grenadier Mohammad Naseem.

The Battle of Phillora, the largest tank battle fought after World War II, was recreated from a long conversation with Brig Jasbir Singh (Retd) and Dfr Vir Singh of 4 Horse and Maj Gen Kartick Ganguly (Retd) from 5/9 Gorkha Rifles.

The account of the Battle of Barki and the profile of late Sub Ajit Singh were based on interviews with Col Manmohan Singh (Retd) from 16 Punjab, and Brig Kanwaljit Singh (Retd) and Col Baldev Singh Chahal (Retd) from 4 Sikh.

The account of the Battle of Dograi was written from interviews with Maj Gen B.R. Varma (Retd), AVSM, who was 3 Jat Adjutant in 1965; and Col Durjan Singh Shekhawat (Retd), who was battalion 2IC. Personal touches were added to the profile of Brig Desmond E. Hayde, MVC, after conversations with Lt Col Kunwar Ajay Singh (Retd), who runs the late Brigadier's dream project, Heritage Academy, in Kotdwar.

Select Bibliography

Ganguly, Major General Kartick (Retd). 2014. *Moments of Maximum Danger: The Odyssey of an Indian Soldier*. Kolkata: Smriti Publishers.

Hayde, Brigadier Desmond E. (Retd). 2011. *The Battle of Dograi and Batapore*. Dehradun: Natraj Publishers.

Lehl, Major General Lachhman Singh. 1997. *Missed Opportunities: Indo-Pak War 1965*. Dehradun: Natraj Publishers.

Pradhan, R.D. 2007. *1965 War: The Inside Story—Defence Minister Y.B. Chavan's Diary of India-Pakistan War*. New Delhi: Atlantic Publishers & Dist.

Prasad, S.N. and U.P. Thapliyal (eds). 2011. *The India-Pakistan War of 1965: A History*. New Delhi: Ministry of Defence, Government of India.

Praval, K.C. 1975. *India's Paratroopers: A History of the Parachute Regiment of India*. London: Leo Cooper.

Raghavan, Brigadier V.R. 2002. *By Land and Sea: The Post-Independence History of the Punjab Regiment 1947–86*, vol. 2. New Delhi: Lancer Publishers.

Singh, Colonel Bhupinder. 1982. *1965 War: Role of Tanks in India–Pakistan War*. Patiala: B.C. Publishers.

Singh, Colonel Kanwaljit and Major H.S. Ahluwalia. 1987. *Saragarhi Battalion: Ashes to Glory.* New Delhi: Lancer.

Singh, Lieutenant General Hanut (Retd). 1993. *Fakhr-E-Hind: The Story of the Poona Horse.* Dehradun: Agrim Publishers.

Singh, Lieutenant General Harbaksh. 1991. *War Despatches: Indo-Pak Conflict 1965.* New Delhi/Atlanta: Lancer.

(L-R) Maj H.A. Patil, Capt P.V. Joshi, Maj K.V. Vaswani, Capt D'Souza, Lt Col Prabhjinder Singh, Commanding Officer 1 Para, Maj R.S. Dyal, Capt J.S. Bindra and Capt M.M.P.S. Dhillon. Officers of 1 Para after the capture of Haji Pir Pass.

Union Minister for Information and Broadcasting Indira Gandhi addressing villagers at Haji Pir.

Pakistani POWs during the 1971 war, one of whom harked back to 1965 and told Maj Arvinder Singh, '*Tussi Major de Major hi reh gaye, main te Lance Naik se Havildar ban gaya* (You have remained a Major, while I've become a Havildar from a Lance Naik).'

Army Chief Gen J. N. Chaudhuri, OBE, addressing officers and jawans at the 4 Grenadiers battle location near Chima village.

Troops being addressed before the Battle of Asal Uttar.

A foxhole bunker used by the Commander
of Charlie Coy in Asal Uttar.

Intrepid soldiers of 4 Grenadiers.

Lt H.R. Janu and Capt Surender Chowdhary, Adjutant,
4 Grenadiers, relaxing during a lull in the war.

Lt Janu standing atop a Patton tank
destroyed by his company, Charlie Coy.

A captured Patton tank.

A Pakistani Patton tank captured in the war,
now displayed at Jabalpur cantonment.

Destroyed enemy tanks lined up on the Road Khem Karan–Bhikhiwind.

NEVER IN THE HISTORY OF WARFARE HAVE SO MANY TANKS BEEN DESTROYED
BY ANY INFANTRY MAN-A FEAT ACHIEVED BY CQMH ABDUL HAMID OF 4 GRENADIERS
WHO DESTROYED EIGHT PAKISTANI PATTON TANKS WITH
THIS 106 RECOILESS GUN BEFORE LAYING DOWN HIS LIFE FOR THE NATION
HE WAS AWARDED PARAM VIR CHAKRA POSTHUMOUSLY FOR HIS DARING ACT.
"SARVADA SHAKTISHALI"

CQMH Abdul Hamid's act of valour documented on a plaque.

CQMH Hamid's jeep.

Grenadiers laying a *chadar* at the *mazar* of CQMH Hamid.

Bust of CQMH Hamid at the Grenadiers Regimental Centre.

Captured intact on the Libbe–Phillora road, this Patton tank, along with four other Pattons, had earlier shot and destroyed Dfr Prithipal Singh's tank.

The 17 Horse Squadron Commander's tank, Nalua, enters Phillora Police Station.

The Phillora Police Station sign.

Maj Govind Singh along with Other Ranks of Bravo
Squadron, 4 Horse, at Phillora Police Station.

Troops with a destroyed Patton tank. (Standing L–R) Lt Col K. Rishi
Raj Singh (Commandant), Ris Maj Jagir Singh (Retd), Maj Gen K. Jang
Shamsher Singh (Colonel of the regiment) with other officers and men.

Maj Gen K. Jang Shamsher Singh on a visit to the operations
area after the ceasefire of 1965. In the background is a
Pakistani M48 tank knocked down by Poona Horse.

Officers of Charlie Squadron of Poona Horse. (L–R) Lt V. Patil, Maj V. Singh, Capt M.L. Dar (he replaced Capt Ajai Singh after the operations) and Lt V.K. Kapoor.

Capt K. Khanna (extreme left) and other regiment officers of 4 Horse.

De-induction of 4 Horse after the 1965 operations.

Troops after the capture of the objective, Barki.

Destroyed Patton tanks lined up near Barki.

A damaged enemy tank.

Barki Police Station captured by Delta Company of 4 Sikh.

Soldiers of 4 Sikh atop a pillbox in Barki.

President Sarvepalli Radhakrishnan meeting troops.

The blown-up bridge at Ichhogil Canal; 3 Jat has the rare distinction of crossing the formidable enemy obstacle system twice.

The Tricolour proudly hoisted atop a pillbox at Dograi. Jats do the nation proud.

Dead bodies of Pakistani soldiers being loaded on to a truck.

Officers and Junior Commissioned Officers of 54 Infantry Brigade
with their Commander, Brig Niranjan Singh.

Maharaja of Patiala and Brig Niranjan Singh standing with Commanding
Officers and Other Ranks in front of a captured Pakistani Patton tank.

Brig Niranjan Singh, MC, being introduced to Prime Minister
Lal Bahadur Shastri on GT Road in front of the Pakistan custom house.

Prime Minister Shastri congratulating
Lt Col D.E. Hayde, Commanding Officer, 3 Jat.

Prime Minister Shastri addressing the victorious troops.

Lt Col Hayde with Defence Minister Y.B. Chavan.

The bullet-riddled helmet of Capt K.S. Thapa, MVC.

A bullet hole in a Commanding Officer's water bottle.

This milestone was brought back by 3 Jat
as a memento; they were 13 miles from Lahore.

The victorious Jats at Amritsar.

Gallant Jats marching through the streets of Amritsar.

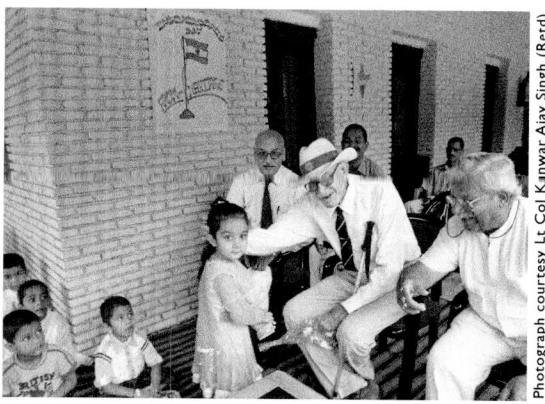

Brig Hayde (wearing a hat) interacting with children at Heritage Academy, Kotdwar, the school that was established on land he donated.